P0R
1792

HARD·BOILED

Great Lines from

Classic Noir Films

DO NOT PLACE FINE MONEY IN BOOK.
FINES TO BE PAID AT DESK.

HARD·BOILED

Great Lines from
Classic Noir Films

with an introduction by
LEE SERVER

Peggy Thompson and
Saeko Usukawa

CHRONICLE BOOKS
SAN FRANCISCO

Printed in Hong Kong.

Library of Congress Cataloging-in Publication Data

Thompson, Peggy, 1952–
    Hard-boiled : great lines from classic noir films / Peggy Thompson and Saeko Usukawa.
        p. cm.
    Includes index.
    ISBN 0-8118-0855-6
    1. Film noir—Quotations, maxims, etc.
    I. Usukawa, Saeko, 1946–
    II. Title.
PN1995.9.F54T56 1996
791.43'655—dc20   94-48310
                                       CIP

Distributed in Canada by Raincoast Books
8680 Cambie Street
Vancouver, BC V6P 6M9

10 9 8 7 6 5 4 3 2 1

Chronicle Books
275 Fifth Street
San Francisco, CA 94103

Book and cover design: Barbara Hodgson/ Byzantium Books
Composition: Byzantium Books

Front cover photograph: *Fallen Angel* (1946). Back cover photographs (from top to bottom): *The Big Combo* (1955), *The Big Steal* (1949), and *Sleep, My Love* (1948).

Page ii: Ex-con Joe Gargan (George Raft) avenges the murder of his brother-in-law by loan shark racketeers in a brutal showdown that ends with a particularly gruesome death in the low-budget but menacing *Loan Shark* (1952).

Previous spread: Finally pushed over the edge, the obliging Christopher Cross (Edward G. Robinson), here wearing an apron and brandishing a knife, turns on his nagging wife Adele (Rosalind Ivan) in *Scarlet Street* (1945).

Facing page: Escaped gangster Joe Sullivan (Dennis O'Keefe) is wounded in the stomach, at bay with girlfriend Ann Martin (Marsha Hunt), whom he's seduced into his shadowy, nightmarish world in *Raw Deal* (1948).

We thank the following people for their research, help, advice, support and loans from their collections: Schroeder, Alain Silver and Elizabeth Ward (authors of the invaluable *Film Noir: An Encyclopedic Reference to the American Style*), John Teegarden and Dale Nash, Jane Cloud and Justin Caulder of Captain Video, Dennis Mills and Michelle Normoyle, Janet Lorenz. We are also grateful to our agents and designers, Barbara Hodgson and Nick Bantock of Byzantium Books, and to our editor Annie Barrows and her assistant Karen Silver at Chronicle Books, as well as to proofreader Ellen Klages who saved us from ourselves.

Stills and lobby cards from the following are used by permission of Turner Entertainment Co.: *Angel Face* ©1953 RKO Pictures Inc. All Rights Reserved; *Beyond the Forest* ©1949 Turner Entertainment Co. All Rights Reserved; *Born to Kill* ©1947 RKO Pictures Inc. All rights Reserved; *Dark Passage* ©1947 Turner Entertainment Co. All Rights Reserved; *His Kind of Woman* ©1951 RKO Pictures Inc. All Rights Reserved; *Macao* ©1952 RKO Pictures Inc. All Rights Reserved; *The Racket* ©1951 RKO Pictures Inc. All Rights Reserved; *They Won't Believe Me* ©1947 RKO Pictures Inc. All Rights Reserved.

Screenwriters: *Affair in Trinidad:* Oscar Saul, James Gunn/*Angel Face:* Frank Nugent, Oscar Millar, Chester Erskine story/*The Asphalt Jungle:* Ben Maddow, John Huston, W.R. Burnett novel/*Beyond a Reasonable Doubt:* Douglas Morrow/*Beyond the Forest:* Lenore Coffee/*Beware My Lovely:* Mel Dinelli/*The Big Carnival:* Billy Wilder, Lesser Samuels, Walter Newman/*The Big Clock:* Jonathan Latimer, Harold Goldman, Kenneth Fearing novel/*The Big Combo:* Philip Yordan/*The Big Heat:* Sydney Boehm, William P. McGivern novel/*The Big Sleep:* William Faulkner, Leigh Bracket, Jules Furthman, Raymond Chandler novel/*The Big Steal:* Gerald Drayson Adams, Geoffrey Homes/*The Blue Dahlia:* Raymond Chandler/*Body and Soul:* Abraham Polonsky/*Born to Kill:* Eve Greene, Richard Macauley/*The Brothers Rico:* Lewis Meltzer, Ben Perry, Georges Simenon novel/*Calcutta:* Seton I. Miller/*Cape Fear:* James R. Webb, John D. MacDonald novel/*Casablanca:* Julius J. Epstein, Philip G. Epstein, Howard Koch/*Caught:* Arthur Laurents/*Christmas Holiday:* Herman J. Mankiewicz, Somerset Maugham novel/*City Across the River:* Maxwell Shane, Dennis Cooper, Irving Shulman novel/*Clash by Night:* Alfred Hayes, Clifford Odets play/*Crack-Up:* John Paxton/*Criss Cross:* Daniel Fuchs/*Crossfire:* John Paxton/*Cry Danger:* William Bowers/*Cry of the City:* Richard Murphy/*The Dark Corner:* Jay Drather, Bernard Schoenfeld, Leo Rosten story/*The Dark Mirror:* Nunnally Johnson/*Dark Passage:* Delmer Daves, David Goodis novel/*Dead Reckoning:* Oliver Garrett, Steve Fisher, Allen Rivkin/*Detour:* Martin Goldsmith/*D.O.A.:* Russell Rouse, Clarence Greene/*Double Indemnity:* Raymond Chandler, Billy Wilder, James M. Cain novel/*A Double Life:* Ruth Gordon, Garson Kanin/*The Enforcer:* Martin Rackin/*Experiment in Terror:* Gordon and Mildred Gordon/*Fallen Angel:* Harry Kleiner/*The Fallen Sparrow:* Warren Duff, Dorothy B. Hughes novel/*The Female Jungle:* Burt Kaiser, Bruno Ve Sota/*The File on Thelma Jordan:* Ketti Frings/*Follow Me Quietly:* Lillie Hayward, Francis Rosenwald, Anthony Mann story/*Force of Evil:* Abraham Polonsky, Ira Wolfert/*The Gangster:* Daniel Fuchs/*Gilda:* Marion Parsonnet, Jo Eisinger/*The Glass Key:* Jonathan Latimer, Dashiell Hammett novel/*Gun Crazy:* Mackinlay Kantor, Millard Kaufman, Dalton Trumbo/*He Walked by Night:* John C. Higgins, Crane Wilbur/*High Sierra:* John Huston, W. R. Burnett novel/*His Kind of Woman:* Frank Fenton, Jack Leonard/*Hollow Triumph:* Daniel Fuchs/*Hoodlum Empire:* Bruce Manning, Bob Considine/*I Am a Fugitive from a Chain Gang:* Howard J. Greene, Brown Holmes/*I Wake Up Screaming:* Dwight Taylor, Steve Fisher novel/*Impact:* Dorothy Reid/*In a Lonely Place:* Andrew Solt, Edmund H. North, Dorothy B. Hughes novel/*Journey into Fear:* Joseph Cotten, Orson Welles, Eric Ambler novel/*Key Largo:* Richard Brooks, John Huston, Maxwell Anderson play/*The Killers:* Anthony Veiller, Ernest Hemingway story/*The Killing:* Stanley Kubrick, Jim Thompson/*Kiss Me Deadly:* A.I. Bezzerides, Mickey Spillane novel/*Kiss of Death:* Ben Hecht, Charles Lederer/*Knock on Any Door:* Daniel Taradash, John Monks, Jr./*Lady from Shanghai:* Orson Welles/*Lady in the Lake:* Steve Fisher, Raymond Chandler novel/*Laura:* Jay Dratler, Samuel Hoffenstein, Betty Reinhardt/*The Lost Weekend:* Charles Brackett, Billy Wilder, Charles Jackson novel/*Macao:* Bernard C. Schoenfeld, Stanley Rubin/*The Maltese Falcon:* John Huston, Dashiell Hammett novel/*The Manchurian Candidate:* George Axelrod, John Frankenheimer, Richard Condon novel/*Marked Woman:* Robert Rossen, Abem Finkel/*Mildred Pierce:* Ranald MacDougall, James M. Cain novel/*Moonrise:* Charles Haas/*Murder, My Sweet:* John Paxton, Raymond Chandler novel/*My Gun Is Quick:* Richard Collins, Richard Powell, Mickey Spillane novel/*The Naked City:* Albert Maltz, Malvin Wald/*Naked Kiss:* Samuel Fuller/*The Narrow Margin:* Earl Fenton/*Niagara:* Charles Brackett, Walter Reisch, Richard Breen/*Night and the City:* Jo Eisinger/*Night of the Hunter:* James Agee, Davis Grubb novel/*No Way Out:* Joseph L. Mankiewicz, Lesser Samuels/*Nocturne:* Jonathan Latimer/*Notorious:* Ben Hecht/*On Dangerous Ground:* A. I. Bezzerides, Nicholas Ray/*Out of the Past:* Geoffrey Homes, Frank Fenton/*Panic in the Streets:* Richard Murphy, Daniel Fuchs/*The Paradine Case:* David O. Selznick/*Party Girl:* George Wells/*The Petrified Forest:* Charles Kenyon, Delmer Daves, Robert Sherwood play/*Phantom Lady:* Bernard Schoenfeld, William Irish (Cornell Woolrich) novel/*Pickup on South Street:* Samuel Fuller/*The Pitfall:* Karl Kamb/*A Place in the Sun:* Michael Wilson, Harry Brown, Theodore Dreiser novel/*Plunder Road:* Steven Ritch, Jack Charney/*The Postman Always Rings Twice:* Harry Ruskin, Niven Busch, James M. Cain novel/*The Prowler:* Hugo Butler, Dalton Trumbo/*Pushover:* Roy Huggins/*The Racket:* William Wister Haines, W. R. Burnett/*Raw Deal:* Leopold Atlas, John C. Higgins/*Riffraff:* Martin Rackin/*Road House:* Edward Chodorov/*Scarlet Street:* Dudley Nichols/*The Second Woman:* Robert Smith, Mort Briskin/*Shadow of a Doubt:* Thornton Wilder, Sally Benson, Alma Reville, Gordon McDonell story/*Shanghai Express:* Jules Furthman/*The Shanghai Gesture:* Josef von Sternberg, Karl Vollmoeller, Geza Herczeg, Jules Furthman/*Shock Corridor:* Samuel Fuller/*Singapore:* Seton I. Miller, Robert Thoeren/*Slaughter on Tenth Avenue:* Lawrence Roman/*Sleep, My Love:* St. Clair McKelway, Leo Rosten/*Sorry, Wrong Number:* Lucille Fletcher/*Spellbound:* Ben Hecht, Angus MacPhail/*The Spiral Staircase:* Mel Dinelli/*The Steel Trap:* Andrew Stone/*The Strange Love of Martha Ivers:* Robert Rossen/*The Stranger:* Anthony Veiller/*Stranger on the Third Floor:* Frank Partos/*Strangers on a Train:* Raymond Chandler, Czenzi Ormonde, Whitfield Cook, Patricia Highsmith novel/*The Street with No Name:* Harry Kleiner, Robert Smith/*Sudden Fear:* Lenore Coffee, Robert Smith/*Suddenly:* Richard Sale/*Sunset Boulevard:* Charles Brackett, Billy Wilder, D. M. Marshman, Jr./*Sweet Smell of Success:* Clifford Odets, Ernest Lehman/*They Drive by Night:* Jerry Wald, Richard Macaulay, A.I. Bezzerides novel/*They Live by Night:* Charles Schnee, Nicholas Ray/*They Won't Believe Me:* Jonathan Latimer, Gordon McDonell story/*The Thin Man:* Frances Goodrich, Albert Hackett, Dashiell Hammett novel/*The Third Man:* Graham Greene/*This Gun for Hire:* Albert Maltz, W. R. Burnett, Graham Greene novel/*To Have and Have Not:* Jules Furthman, William Faulkner, Ernest Hemingway novel/*Touch of Evil:* Orson Welles/*Uncle Harry:* Stephen Longstreet, Keith Winter/*Undercurrent:* Edward Chodorov/*Underworld Story:* Henry Blankfort/*Underworld U.S.A.:* Samuel Fuller/*The Uninvited:* Dodie Smith/*Vertigo:* Alec Coppel, Samuel Taylor/*The Web:* William Bowers, Bertram Millhauser/*When Strangers Marry:* Philip Yordan, Dennis J. Cooper/*While the City Sleeps:* Casey Robinson/*White Heat:* Ivan Goff, Ben Roberts, Virginia Kellogg story/*The Window:* Mel Dinelli, William Irish (Cornell Woolrich) novelette/*The Woman in the Window:* Nunnally Johnson/*You Only Live Once:* Gene Towne, Graham Baker.

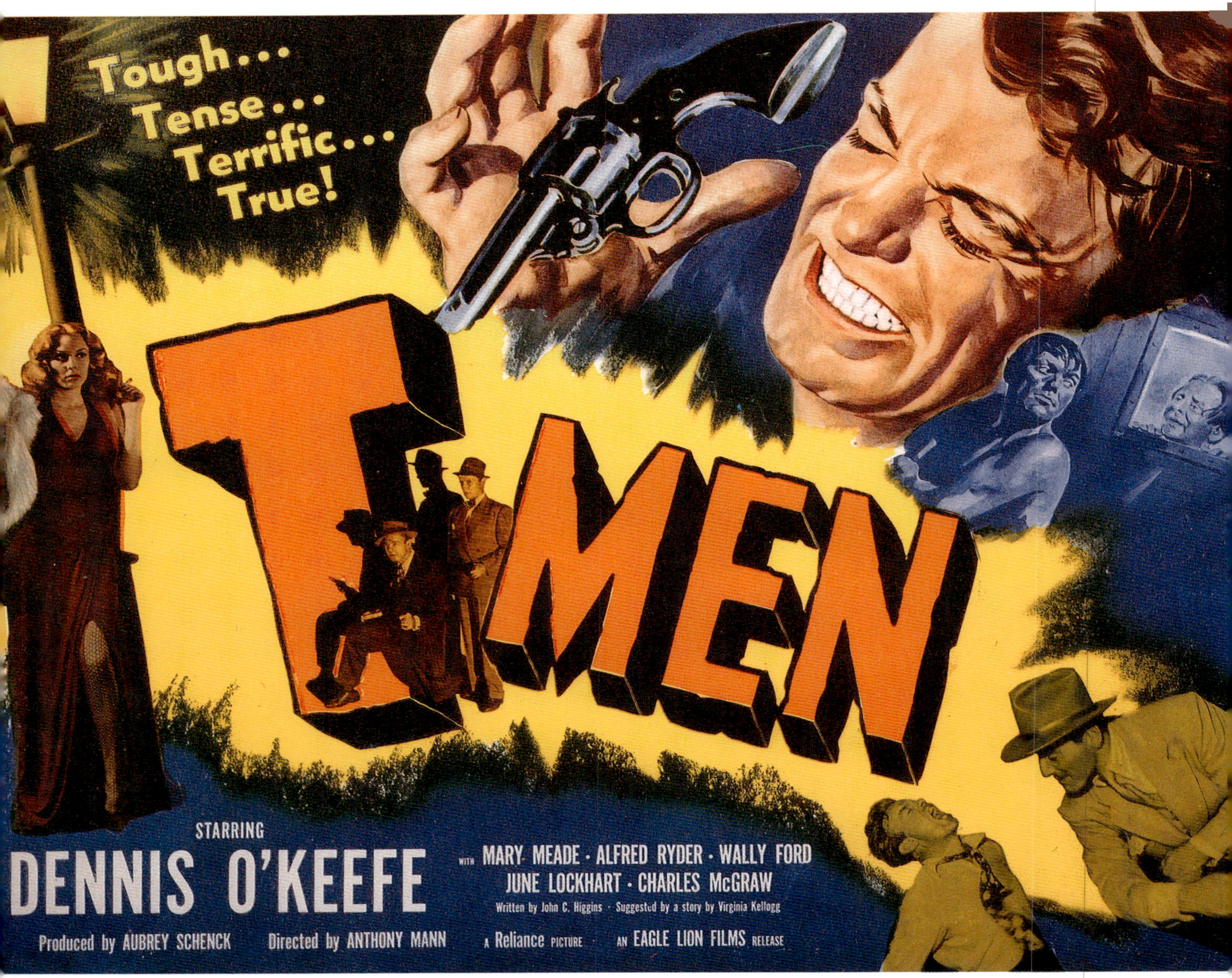
Tough...
Tense...
Terrific...
True!
T-MEN
STARRING
DENNIS O'KEEFE
WITH MARY MEADE · ALFRED RYDER · WALLY FORD
JUNE LOCKHART · CHARLES McGRAW
Written by John C. Higgins · Suggested by a story by Virginia Kellogg
Produced by AUBREY SCHENCK
Directed by ANTHONY MANN
A Reliance PICTURE
AN EAGLE LION FILMS RELEASE

HARD·BOILED

Introduction *by Lee Server*

This is film noir: two silhouetted hit men in overcoats and fedoras approaching a New Jersey diner like messengers from Hell. Burt Lancaster in the same movie, lying in bed waiting to be killed, saying, "I did something wrong . . . Once." Noir is Tom Neal ruminating on the soundtrack about Fate putting the finger on you or me for no good reason at all and Rita Hayworth's Gilda purring, "If I'd been a ranch, they would have named me the Bar Nothing." It's Orson Welles's corrupt cop wanting his future read and brothel owner Marlene Dietrich telling him, "You haven't got any . . . your future is all used up."

Classic film noir is a matter of three hundred or so titles produced between 1940 and 1960. The term was first used in Paris in 1946, when French cineastes were catching up with the Hollywood product of the war years. In among the Betty Grable musicals and Abbott and Costello slapstick was a vein of harsh, downbeat crime stories. The dark tone, the violence and misanthropy in these films made them seem very much the blood brothers of the hard-boiled American fiction—by authors like Dashiell Hammett, James M. Cain, W. R. Burnett— being published in a new line of French paperbacks called *Serie Noire*.

An antisocial corrective to the Hollywood of candy-colored optimism and Andy Hardy values, these "black films" presented a world of fear, paranoia, and infinite corruption. Heroes were opportunists, or victims, or both—drifters, seedy private eyes, gunsels. Heroines were alluring, available, and deadly. Cops were crooked, institutions were evil, and best friends were likely to shoot you in the back. The setting was a sordid, Technicolor-free America, an urban jungle made up entirely of cheap hotels with flashing neon signs, greasy spoon diners, alleyways, gambling joints, and police interrogation rooms. Instead of the traditional Hollywood happy ending, there was the wailing siren of a squad car closing

Opposite: Treasury agent Dennis O'Brien (Dennis O'Keefe) goes undercover to join a counterfeiting ring and is forced to stand by helplessly while they gun down his partner in *T Men* (1948), the first successful picture for director Anthony Mann, who went on to direct other noirs, including *Raw Deal*, and many noir westerns.

in or the bullet fired at close range. And all of it photographed in shadow-haunted images of an extravagant stylization.

The French critics had tapped into the emergence of a Hollywood genre that Hollywood itself had not yet recognized as such. The movies in question had been variously produced and promoted as gangster pictures, women's pictures, mysteries. Only in retrospect was it clear how much they shared in characters, themes, style, iconography. *Noir* categorized them precisely and evocatively.

Trying to determine the first film noir is a properly murky business. Some point to a 1940 B movie, *Stranger on the Third Floor,* as the most likely suspect. Directed by Boris Ingster from a script by Frank Partos (with uncredited contributions from Nathanael West no less), *Stranger* is about a newspaper reporter whose righteous testimony puts an accused murderer on Death Row. But then he starts to think someone else was the actual killer—maybe popeyed stranger Peter Lorre—and he is painfully correct. A neighbor is killed, and this time the reporter himself is accused of the crime. *Stranger* is noir all right, with its "wrong man" theme, paranoid hero, and expressionist dream sequence, but the film appears to have had no influence whatever at the time of its release. If this is the first film noir, its significance is primarily archaeological. One might just as well give the honor to any of a number of "prematurely" noir productions: *Underworld, Pandora's Box, Scarface, Le Jour se leve, Les Vampires, Blood Money,* or the Complete Works of Fritz Lang.

The true catalysts for the genre are two 1941 releases by a pair of young Americans making their directorial debuts. The phantasmagoric visuals and complex narrative of Orson Welles's *Citizen Kane* would cause a quiet revolution among Hollywood writers,

Above: The mysterious, menacing Peter Lorre played prototypical noir characters in a number of films, including *Stranger on the Third Floor, The Mask of Dimitrios, Quicksand,* and the classic *The Maltese Falcon.*

directors, and cinematographers. Mainstream moviemaking had developed in the '30s a seamless, self-effacingly naturalistic style that *Kane* exploded in a torrent of expressionist and avant-garde effects. *Kane's* fractured form of storytelling was equally innovative; a web of flashbacks, symbols, shifting viewpoints. Film noir, in particular the baroque "high noir" style of the mid to late '40s, was where these visual and narrative innovations would flourish. *The Killers*, directed by Robert Siodmak (scripted by John Huston and Anthony Veiller), for example, was a virtual replication of *Kane* as a hard-boiled thriller. And, of course, Orson Welles would eventually bring his style to the genre in person, directing two of the greatest and most representative of film noirs, *The Lady from Shanghai* and *Touch of Evil*.

In contrast to *Citizen Kane's* high-profile release, *The Maltese Falcon* came out with little fanfare but would prove to be an unexpected sensation, the sleeper of the year. Dashiell Hammett's 1930 private eye novel had already been filmed twice to little effect (once as a comedy) when John Huston begged Jack Warner to let him remake it. They say that Huston "filmed the book" but history has shown that to be something easier said than done. Hammett's novel was perfect, which only left Huston to cast the roles with a group of newcomers and also-rans, pace the action as tightly as a clenched fist, and write a poetic last line (Hammett's novel was too stoic for such things) that would chill the spine. Simple.

The Maltese Falcon did nothing less than reinvent the Hollywood crime movie. In the early '30s, crime pictures had been effectively run out of town by the Joe Breen Gang, the Production Code censors. Attempts to put gangsters back on screen generally provoked cries of protest. Mysteries, on the other hand, had evolved into bloodless affairs with lighthearted detectives like Nick Charles and The Saint. *The Maltese Falcon* was a revelation to Hollywood—a way to tell a mystery story with the drama and ferocity of a gangster picture. Success breeds imitation and elements of Huston's work—the nocturnal settings, the ambivalently ethical hero, the femme fatale, the cynical worldview—would be endlessly echoed in the film noirs to come.

Next page: New Orleans police detective René Brossard (Edward G. Robinson) gets tangled up with murder, dreams, hypnosis, and clever disguise in *Nightmare* (1956), director Maxwell Shane's remake of his 1947 version of the same story, *Fear in the Night*. Both films feature dream sequences and murders in mirrored rooms.

To be sure, the genre was ultimately shaped by any number of influences: the nightmarish novels of Cornell Woolrich, an assortment of UFA-trained filmmakers, radio suspense programs, the popularization of psychiatry, wartime anxiety, Cold War paranoia, and so on. From *Falcon's* relatively lucid, straight-ahead approach, film noir evolved into something considerably more convoluted, bleak, and strange. Noir kicked into overdrive in 1944, the year of *Double Indemnity*, *Laura*, *Phantom Lady*, and *Murder, My Sweet*. The great critical and commercial success of *Double Indemnity*, in particular, would prove decisive. Here was a film wherein the male and female leads were attractive, cold-blooded murderers. The gloves were off and the censors were reeling. Noir turned a darker shade of black, reveling in sociopathy. The studios went into production with properties that had once been considered too hot to handle—*The Postman Always Rings Twice*, *Leave Her to Heaven*, *Nightmare Alley*. Films like *Born to Kill*—with Lawrence Tierney and sister-in-law Claire Trevor becoming sexually aroused over memories of a bloody double homicide—reached a level of depravity previously unknown in commercial cinema.

As these movies increasingly dealt with aberrant behavior and exotic states of mind—schizophrenia, amnesia, kleptomania, even (in *Street With No Name*) a particularly virulent case of hypochondria—their form became similarly "deranged," containing hallucinatory visuals and labyrinthine plots, dream sequences, and flashbacks within flashbacks. Noir's radical nature encouraged experimentally-inclined filmmakers like Welles and Hitchcock, and brought out the latent adventurousness in Hollywood professionals like Joseph H. Lewis, director of the extraordinary one-take robbery sequence in *Gun Crazy*.

Noir's peak of popularity came in the years after World War II. Every major and minor studio produced its share of dark

Above: A studio publicity photo of James Cagney, who often played tough, cocky characters in the 1930s and 1940s. He gave a bravura performance as the psychopathic gangster Cody Jarrett in the film *White Heat* (1949).

melodramas, and some, like Eagle-Lion, seemed to produce nothing else. Noir's influence was pervasive, extending across generic borders to infect the Western and the war film, and even the musical *(Red Hot and Blue)* and the historical (Philip Yordan and Anthony Mann's *The Black Book*, aka *Reign of Terror,* the only film noir about the French Revolution). Some of the greatest examples of the genre appeared in the 1950s—*Pickup on South Street, The Big Combo, Kiss Me Deadly*—but the popular interest in noir began to flag in the face of wide screen and color, though films like *House of Bamboo* and *I Died a Thousand Times* proved great noirs could be made in these processes. The classic period was over by the end of the decade. Noir died, however, with a bang worthy of *White Heat's* Cody Jarrett: a pair of supreme achievements in Welles's *Touch of Evil* and Alfred Hitchcock's *Vertigo.* After these two, nothing, really, remained to be said.

The following pages are a tribute in the form of a scrapbook, a selection of memorable words and pictures drawn from the glory days of film noir. They offer an alluring glimpse at the images created by the pantheon of noir directors—Siodmak, Mann, Welles, Huston, Lang, Lewis, Sam Fuller, Otto Preminger, et al—and cinematographers who specialized in this world of shadows—John Alton, Woody Bredell, Joseph LaShelle, and the rest. Even more, these pages afford the chance to reappraise the great dialogue of film noir, the hard-boiled poetry and wit of the too-often neglected screenwriters and masters of the form like Philip Yordan and Harry Kleiner, Ben Hecht, A.I. Bezzerides, and many more.

   If these films are unfamiliar then let this book serve as an introduction to one of the great chapters in the history of the movies, and a "coming attraction" for the pleasures that await you.

Affair in Trinidad 1952

"When did you last see your husband?"
"At breakfast—why?"
"Did you talk to him?"
"Sure. I asked him to pass me the salt."
—*Torin Thatcher (police inspector Smythe) and Rita Hayworth (chanteuse Chris Emery)*

"No one can live on grief. Yesterday is yesterday, tomorrow is tomorrow."
"You left out today,"
"Today is already yesterday."
—*Juanita Moore (housekeeper Dominique) and Rita Hayworth (her boss, chanteuse Chris Emery)*

"Veronica, some people are mellowed by drink. I suggest you have another."
—*Alexander Scourby (German spymaster Max Fabian) to Valerie Bettis (alcoholic spy Veronica)*

Angel Face 1953

"You know something— you're a pretty nice guy, for a girl."
—*Robert Mitchum (ambulance driver Frank Jessup)*

"I'd say your story was as phony as a three-dollar bill."
"How can you say that to me?"
"You mean after all that we've been to each other?"
—*Robert Mitchum (ambulance driver Frank Jessup) and Jean Simmons (femme fatale Diane Tremayne)*

"If you want to play with matches, that's your business. But not in gas-filled rooms."
—*Robert Mitchum (ambulance driver Frank Jessup) to Jean Simmons (femme fatale Diane Tremayne)*

Opposite: A bartender (bit player) serves the murderous, upper-class femme fatale Diane Tremayne (Jean Simmons) and her lover, chauffeur Frank Jessup (Robert Mitchum), in Otto Preminger's *Angel Face* (1953).

9

The Asphalt Jungle 1950

"Crime is a left-handed form of human endeavor."
—*Sam Jaffe (ex-con Doc Riedenschneider)*

"If you want fresh air, don't look for it in this town."
—*Anthony Caruso (safecracker Louis Ciavelli)*

"You big boys, what've you got? Front, nothing but front."
—*Brad Dexter (Bob Brannon)*

Beyond a Reasonable Doubt 1956

"I've never seen your apartment."
"Isn't that supposed to be my line?"
"But you've never used it."
—*Joan Fontaine (heiress Susan Spencer) and Dana Andrews (her fiancé, novelist Tom Garrett)*

Beyond the Forest 1949

"This is the story of evil. Evil is headstrong, is puffed up. For our souls' sake, it is salutary for us to view it in all its naked ugliness once in a while. Thus may we know how those who deliver themselves over to it end up like the Scorpion, in a mad frenzy stinging themselves to eternal death."
—*title at the top of the movie*

"Life in Loyalton is like sitting in a funeral parlor waiting for the funeral to begin."
—*Bette Davis (unhappily married Rosa Moline) to Minor Watson (her husband's friend Moose)*

"Anything I had to say to you, I wouldn't put on paper."
—*David Brian (millionaire Neil Latimer) to Bette Davis (his lover Rosa Moline)*

Opposite: Bette Davis is one of the baddest and most warped of all the femmes fatales in noir as the discontented and money-hungry Rosa Moline in the over-the-top *Beyond the Forest* (1949), with a screenplay by the prolific Lenore Coffee. THE TEEGARDEN/NASH COLLECTION

"WHAT A DUMP!" —*Bette Davis (unhappily married Rosa Moline)*

"I DON'T THINK I EVER LOVED ANYONE. AND I *KNOW* THAT NO ONE EVER LOVED ME."

—Robert Ryan (psychopathic handyman Howard) to Ida Lupino (his employer Mrs. Gordon)

Beware My Lovely 1952

"I haven't seen a dog yet that liked me."

—*Robert Ryan (psychopathic handyman Howard) to Ida Lupino (his employer Mrs. Gordon)*

The Big Carnival
aka Ace in the Hole 1951

"I've done a lot of lying in my time. I've lied to men who wear belts. I've lied to men who wear suspenders. But I'd never be so stupid as to lie to a man who wears both belt and suspenders."

—*Kirk Douglas (ambitious alcoholic reporter Charles Tatum)*

"I've met a lot of hard-boiled eggs in my time, but you— you're twenty minutes."

—*Jan Sterling (Lorraine Minosa) to Kirk Douglas (ambitious alcoholic reporter Charles Tatum)*

"How'd you like to make a thousand dollars a day, Mr. Boot? I'm a thousand-dollar-a-day man. You can have me for nothing."

—*Kirk Douglas (Charles Tatum)*

"I don't pray. Kneeling bags my nylons."

—*Jan Sterling (Lorraine Minosa)*

The Big Clock 1948

"You know, Earl has a passion for obscurity. He won't even have his biography in *Who's Who.*"
"Sure. He doesn't want to let his left hand know whose pocket the right one is picking."

—*Rita Johnson (femme fatale Pauline York) and Ray Milland (crime magazine editor George Stroud) about her keeper and his boss Charles Laughton (Earl Janoth)*

Opposite: The psychotic handyman known only as Howard (Robert Ryan) terrorizes war widow Mrs. Gordon (Ida Lupino) in the late and rather domestic noir *Beware My Lovely* (1952).

13

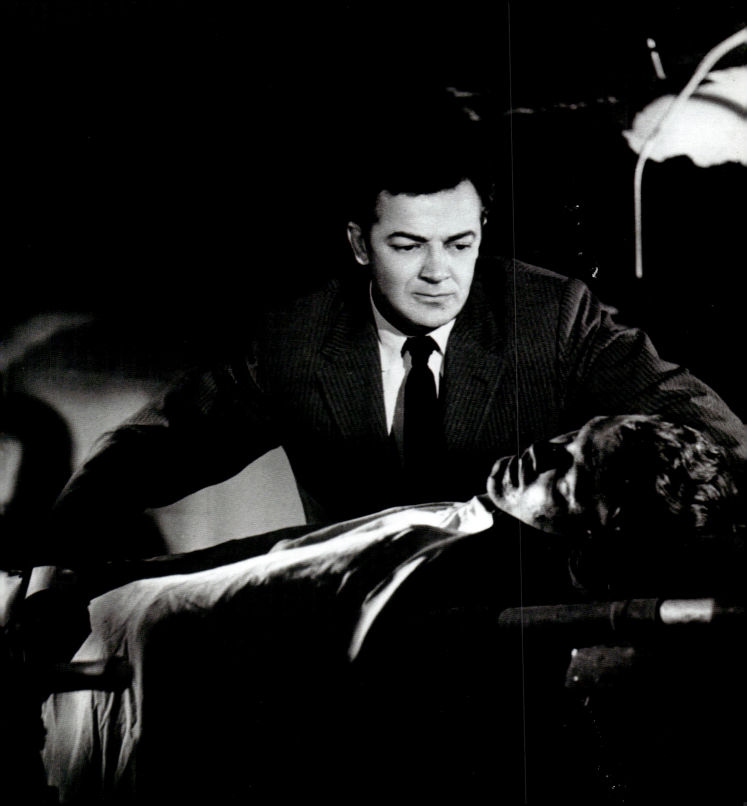

Previous page, left: Overzealous police detective Leonard Diamond (Cornel Wilde) lurks behind Alicia (Helen Walker) in Joseph Lewis's brutal and erotic noir *The Big Combo* (1955). Lewis also directed the cult favorite *Gun Crazy*.

Previous page, right: Police detective Leonard Diamond (Cornel Wilde) examines a body in the morgue in *The Big Combo* which is notable for cinematographer John Alton's classic noir look.

The Big Combo 1955

"It happens to be against two laws, God's and man's. I'm booking her on the second."
—*Cornel Wilde (detective Leonard Diamond)*

"Book me, small change."
—*Richard Conte (gang leader Mr. Brown) to Cornel Wilde (detective Leonard Diamond)*

"What's on your mind? As if I didn't know."
—*Helene Stanton (Rita) to Cornel Wilde (detective Leonard Diamond)*

"Shoots me with my own gun, that's what gets me."
—*Earl Holliman (hit man Mingo)*

"I treated her like a pair of gloves. When I was cold, I called her up."
—*Cornel Wilde (detective Leonard Diamond) about his girlfriend*

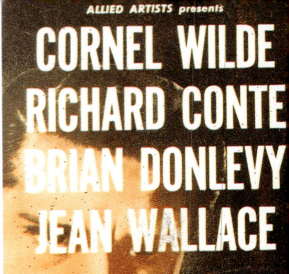

ALLIED ARTISTS presents

CORNEL WILDE
RICHARD CONTE
BRIAN DONLEVY
JEAN WALLACE

THE BIG COMBO

Written by PHILIP YORDAN
Produced by SIDNEY HARMON
Directed by JOSEPH LEWIS

The Big Heat 1953

"Hey, that's a nice perfume."
"Something new. Attracts
    mosquitoes and repels men."

—Lee Marvin (gangster Vince Stone)
and Gloria Grahame (his girfriend
Debby Marsh)

"Hey, I like this. Early
nothing."

—Gloria Grahame (gangster moll
Debby Marsh) about a fleabag hotel
room

"We're all sisters under the
mink."

—Gloria Grahame (gangster moll
Debby Marsh) to Jeanette Nolan
(blackmailer Bertha Nolan)

"I've been rich and I've been
poor. Believe me, rich is
better."

—Gloria Grahame (gangster moll
Debby Marsh) to Glenn Ford
(homicide sergeant Dave Bannion)

The Big Sleep 1946

"My, my. Such a lot of guns
around town and so few
brains."

—Humphrey Bogart (private eye
Philip Marlowe)

"I don't mind if you don't
like my manners. I don't like
them myself. They're pretty
bad. I grieve over them on
long winter evenings."

—Humphrey Bogart (private eye
Philip Marlowe) to Lauren Bacall
(client's daughter Vivian Sternwood)

"She was worth a stare, she
was trouble."

—Humphrey Bogart (private eye
Philip Marlowe) about Lauren Bacall
(client's daughter Vivian Sternwood)

Opposite: Robert Mitchum in a detail from a magazine advertisement for *The Big Steal.*

The Big Steal 1949

"What means 'he pulled a
    fast one'?"
"Copped a Sunday."
"Strange language, but
    colorful."
—*Ramon Novarro (Inspector General) and Don Alvarado (police officer)*

"Stop calling me Chiquita.
    You don't say that to girls
    you don't even know."
"Where I learned Spanish,
    you do."
—*Jane Greer (Joan) and Robert Mitchum (Duke Halliday)*

Top: Duke Halliday (Robert Mitchum), implicated in an army payroll heist, knocks out his pursuer, army Captain Blake (William Bendix), on a liner in Vera Cruz harbor. *The Big Steal* (1949) is a chase-comedy-noir directed by the prolific Don Siegel, who also directed *Invasion of the Body Snatchers*—and *Dirty Harry*.

19

The Blue Dahlia 1946

"Bourbon, straight! With a bourbon chaser!"

—*William Bendix (war vet Buzz Wanchek)*

"You call this dump a hotel?"
"That's what the sign says. Fresh sheets every day, they tell me."
"How often do they change the fleas?"

—*Alan Ladd (war vet Johnny Morrison) and desk clerk*

Opposite: *Body and Soul* (1947) is one of the darkest of the many films set in the corrupt world of boxing in the 1940s. John Garfield plays a tough slum kid who slugs his way to the top but refuses to throw the big fight.

"I go where I want to, with anybody I want. I just happen to be that kind of girl."

—*Doris Dowling (good-time girl Helen Morrison) to Alan Ladd (her husband, war vet Johnny Morrison)*

Born to Kill
aka **Deadlier Than the Male** 1947

"My two husbands was turnips!"

—*Esther Howard (landlady Mrs. Kraft)*

"He's the quiet sort, and yet you get a feeling if you step out of line you'd get your teeth kicked down your throat."

—*Isabel Jewell (Laurie Palmer) about Lawrence Tierney (killer Sam Wild)*

"If we're going to carry on a conversation, it'd help for you to talk."

—*Elisha Cook, Jr. (henchman Marty Waterman) to Lawrence Tierney (killer Sam Wild)*

BODY AND SOUL 1947

"IRMA, ARE YOU DECENT?"
"NOT PARTICULARLY— BRING HIM IN."

—*Lilli Palmer (artist Peg Born) and Virginia Gregg (her roommate Irma)*

"HOW DOES IT LOOK, CHARLEY, THE NIGHT BEFORE THE FIGHT, 3 A.M. AND YOU LOADED?"

—*Hazel Brooks (nightclub singer Alice) to John Garfield (boxer Charley Davis)*

"EVERYBODY DIES. BEN, SHORTY, EVEN YOU."
"WHAT'S THE POINT?"
"NO POINT—THAT'S LIFE."

—*William Conrad (fight manager Quinn) and John Garfield (boxer Charley Davis)*

"WHEN I LOSE THE CHAMPION- SHIP, THEY'LL HAVE TO CARRY ME OUT."
"THIS GYM IS FULL OF GUYS WHO WERE CARRIED OUT."

—*John Garfield (boxer Charley Davis) and Lloyd Goff (gambler and fight promoter Roberts)*

The Brothers Rico 1957

"Maybe I'm gonna die. You've got even bigger problems— you're gonna live."
—*James Darren (gangster Johnny Rico) to Richard Conte (his reformed brother Eddie Rico)*

Calcutta 1947

"Man who trust woman walk on duckweed over pond."
—*Alan Ladd (pilot Neale Gordon) to Gail Russell (femme fatale Virginia Moore)*

"You can't just go round killing people whenever the notion strikes you. It's not feasible."
—*Elisha Cook, Jr. (henchman Marty Waterman) to Lawrence Tierney (killer Sam Wild)*

"There's a kind of depravity in you, Sam."
—*Claire Trevor (femme fatale Helen Trent) to Lawrence Tierney (killer Sam Wild)*

Right: Psychotic killer and ladies man Sam Wild (Lawrence Tierney) gets Helen Trent (Claire Trevor) in a clinch while his wife, Georgia Staples (Audrey Long), sees her world crumble before her in *Born to Kill* (1947).

Left: An advertisement for *Born to Kill*, one of the most sexually obsessive and brutal of all noirs.

LAWRENCE **TIERNEY** · WALTER **SLEZAK**

RKO RADIO PICTURES

IN "Born to Kill"

WITH PHILLIP TERRY
AUDREY LONG

Cape Fear 1962

"Why are we going this
    way?"
"Better scenery."
"What do you know about
    scenery? Or beauty? Or
    any of the things that
    really make life worth
    living? You're just an
    animal—coarse,
    muscled, barbaric."
"You keep right on talking,
    honey. I like the way you
    run me down like that."

—*Barrie Chase (Diane) and Robert
Mitchum (psychopath Max Cady)*

"What I like about you is
you're rock bottom. I
wouldn't expect you to
understand this, but it's a
great comfort for a girl to
know she could not possibly
sink any lower."

—*Barrie Chase (Diane) to Robert
Mitchum (psychopath Max Cady)*

Caught 1949

"Any man who goes to a
party like that has just one
idea. And that's one idea too
many for me."

—*Barbara Bel Geddes (model
Leonora Eames) to Ruth Brady (her
roommate Maxine)*

"What do you know about
    me?"
"Oh, I know you're from
    the east."
"New York."
"And I know you're sort of an
    international something."
"Well, that just about
    describes it. What else?"
"And you're rich."
"How rich?"
"Oh, very rich."

—*Robert Ryan (psychotic millionaire
Smith Ohlrig) and Barbara Bel
Geddes (model Leonora Eames)*

CASABLANCA 1942

"I CAME TO CASABLANCA FOR
    THE WATERS."
"BUT WE'RE IN THE MIDDLE
    OF THE DESERT."
"I WAS MISINFORMED."

—*Humphrey Bogart (nightclub owner Rick) and
Claude Rains (Capt. Louis Renault)*

"HOW EXTRAVAGANT YOU ARE,
THROWING AWAY WOMEN LIKE
THAT. SOMEDAY THEY MAY
BE SCARCE."

—*Claude Rains (Capt. Louis Renault)*

Opposite: Charm-school
graduate Leonora Eames
(Barbara Bel Geddes)
thought she'd find happiness
with wealthy Smith Ohlrig
(Robert Ryan) but now that
she realizes he's a twisted
megalomaniac she'd just as
soon he didn't recover from
this psychosomatic attack in
Max Ophuls's perverse
Cinderella story *Caught*
(1949).

Christmas Holiday 1944

"I can still hear them call you guilty, guilty, guilty—and every time they said it, I knew it was meant for me too."
—*Deanna Durbin (chanteuse Abigail Manette) to Gene Kelly (her wastrel husband Robert Manette)*

"When it was all over, a psychoanalyst said that Robert's relations with his mother were pathological."
—*Deanna Durbin (chanteuse Abigail Manette) about Gene Kelly (her wastrel husband Robert Manette)*

"Bad boy meets good girl. Damage estimated at ten thousand dollars."
—*Richard Whorf (Simon Feniman) to Gene Kelly (his friend, wastrel Robert Manette)*

City Across the River 1949

"Never slug a guy while
wearing a good watch. Take
it off first and put it in your
pocket."

—*Al Ramsen (Duke gang member
Benny Wilkes) to Peter Fernandez
(fellow Duke, Frankie Cusack)*

"Look at him—all dressed
up!"
"Do you like the way I
look?"
"I'd rather look like you than
have my legs cut off."

—*snack-stand owner and Joshua
Shelley (Duke gang member Theodore
"Crazy" Parry)*

"That's everything you did
yesterday?"
"No. At night I slept."

—*policeman questioning a Duke
gang member*

Clash by Night 1952

"Why didn't you come home
before?"
"Why didn't I go to China?
Some things you do, some
things you don't."

—*Keith Andes (fisherman Joe Doyle)
and Barbara Stanwyck (his sister
Mae)*

"What do you want, Joe, my
life history? Here it is in four
words: big ideas, small
results."

—*Barbara Stanwyck (Mae Doyle) to
Keith Andes (her brother Joe)*

"I need a drink—what do
you say?"
"I say I need a drink."

—*Robert Ryan (Earl Pfeiffer) and
Barbara Stanwyck (Mae Doyle)*

"Last time I looked, you had
a wife."
"Maybe next time you look,
I won't."
"That's what they all say."

—*Barbara Stanwyck (Mae Doyle)
and Robert Ryan (Earl Pfeiffer)*

Opposite: A veteran down on
his luck, Chuck Scott (Robert
Cummings), helps Lorna
Roman (Michelle Morgan)
escape from her gang leader
husband in *The Chase*
(1946), an expressionist,
dreamlike noir.

Crack-Up 1946

"Face to face with a painting, we shuffle our feet and apologize. We say, 'I don't know much about art, but I know what I like.' Well, why apologize? If knowing what you like is a good enough way to pick out a wife or a house or a pair of shoes, what's wrong with applying the same rule to paintings?"

—Pat O'Brien (art critic/war vet George Steele) giving lecture

Criss Cross 1949

"I shoulda been a better friend. I shoulda stopped you. I shoulda grabbed you by the neck, I shoulda kicked your teeth in. I'm sorry, Steve."

—Stephen McNally (Lt. Pete Ramirez) to Burt Lancaster (armored car guard Steve Thompson)

"Anna. We were married. About two years ago. It lasted seven months. A man eats an apple, gets a piece of the core stuck between his teeth, you know? He tries to work it out with some cellophane off a cigarette pack. What happens? The cellophane gets stuck in there too. Anna. What was the use? I knew one way or the other, somehow I'd wind up seeing her that night."

—voice-over by Burt Lancaster (armored car guard Steve Thompson)

Above: In *Crack-Up* (1946), Pat O'Brien, who was usually cast as a scrappy tough guy, plays against type as an amnesiac art expert who is framed for murder. The movie was based on the short story "Madman's Holiday" by pulp writer Fredric Brown.

Relentless detective, confronted with the most baffling murder case of his career!

Cynical and secretive sergeant . . . did he know more than he dared reveal?

Tough and full of hate . . . but did he have a *special* reason to kill?

Crossfire 1947

"Where does Monty come
    in? What's he done?"
"He's helping Mitch."
"Every time he opens his
    mouth, he hangs him a
    foot higher."

—*soldier and Robert Mitchum (army
Sgt. Keeley)*

"What did you say your
    name was?"
"Ginny—'cause I'm from
    Virginia."

—*George Cooper (soldier Mitchell)
and Gloria Grahame (bar hostess
Ginny)*

Cry Danger 1951

"Well, the place looks lived in."
"Yeah, but by what?"

—*Richard Erdman (Delong) and
Dick Powell (ex-con Rocky Malloy)*

"Darlene, what do you do?"
"Oh, I'm sort of a part-time
    model."

—*Dick Powell (ex-con Rocky Malloy)
and Jean Porter (Darlene)*

"Big men don't scare easy."
"Big men get popped off
    regularly."

—*William Conrad (racketeer Castro)
and Dick Powell (ex-con Rocky
Malloy)*

Above: Detail from magazine advertisement for *Crossfire* (1947), starring (left to right) Robert Young, Robert Mitchum and Robert Ryan, in a film about an anti-Semitic murder.

29

"I can never sleep after I've been shot up, either."
—*Richard Erdman (Delong)*

"You drinking that stuff this early?"
"Listen, darling, when you drink as much as I do, you gotta start early."
—*Jean Porter (Darlene) and Richard Erdman (Delong)*

Top: Wounded in a battle in which he killed a cop, hospitalized Martin Rome (Richard Conte) refuses to tell homicide officer Lieutenant Candella (Victor Mature) the identity of a mystery woman in Robert Siodmak's semi-documentary *Cry of the City* (1948).

Opposite: Ex-con Rocky (Dick Powell) calls on old girlfriend Nancy (Rhonda Fleming), who lives in a trailer park, while searching for the racketeer who framed him and his best friend for murder in the snappy *Cry Danger* (1951).

Cry of the City 1948

"How much money do you make a week?"
"$94.43."
"Did you ever go to Florida for a week, bet $200 on a horse?"
"No, but I sleep nights."
—*Richard Conte (killer Martin Rome) and Victor Mature (police lieutenant Candella)*

RY DANGER
RICHARD ERDMAN • WILLIAM CONRAD
REGIS TOOMEY • JEAN PORTER
ESENTHAL and W. R. FRANK Directed by ROBERT PARRISH
Screenplay by WILLIAM BOWERS From a Story by JEROME CADY

D.O.A. 1950

"I want to report a murder."
"Sit down. Where was the
    murder committed?"
"San Francisco, last night."
"Who was murdered?"
"I was."

—*Edmond O'Brien (accountant*
Frank Bigelow) and bit player
(policeman)

"The way this guy holds onto
a dollar, you'd think they
weren't printing them
anymore."

—*salesman to Edmond O'Brien*
(accountant Frank Bigelow)

"I know what's going on
inside of you, Frank. You're
just like any other man, only
a little more so."

—*Pamela Britton (secretary Paula*
Gibson) to Edmond O'Brien (her
fiancé Frank Bigelow)

Opposite: With only hours to
go before he's a dead man,
Frank Bigelow (Edmond
O'Brien) tries to discover
from Marla Rakubian
(Laurette Luez) who
poisoned him in Rudolph
Maté's *D.O.A.* (1950), based
on a 1931 German film by
Robert Siodmak, *Der Mann,*
Der Seinen Morder Sucht.

32

6

Beverly Campbell · Neville Brand · Lynn Baggett · William Ching · Henry Hart · Laurette Luez · Produced by Leo C. Popkin · Directed by Rudy Maté
Story and Screenplay by Russell Rouse and Clarence Greene · Music Written and Directed by Dimitri Tiomkin · A Harry M. Popkin Production · Released thru United Artists

The Dark Corner 1946

"Quite a turnout, Hardy. Everybody's here."

"Yes. Nauseating mixture of Park Avenue and Broadway. Proves I'm a liberal."

—Constance Collier (Mrs. Ripley) and Clifton Webb (art dealer/ murderer Hardy Cathcart)

"Mr. Galt, I think someone's following us."

"Yeah, I know. Guy in a white suit, about five-foot ten, brown hair, sport shoes, ring on his left pinky. Don't stare back."

"I've never been followed before."

"That's a terrible reflection on American manhood."

—Lucille Ball (secretary Kathleen) and Mark Stevens (her boss, private eye Bradford Galt)

"I probably shan't return before dawn. How I detest the dawn. The grass looks like it's been left out all night."

—Clifton Webb (art dealer/murderer Hardy Cathcart) to Kurt Kreuger (his wife's lover Tony Jardine)

"I can be framed easier than Whistler's mother."

—Mark Stevens (private eye Bradford Galt) to Lucille Ball (his secretary Kathleen)

Dark Mirror 1946

"All women are rivals, fundamentally."

—Lew Ayres (psychiatrist Dr. Scott Elliott)

Opposite: In *The Dark Corner* (1946), private eye Bradford Galt (Mark Stevens), framed for murder, looks at suspect Hardy Cathcart (Clifton Webb), who's looking at a paper with Galt's face on the front page. Henry Hathaway directed many other noirs, including *Kiss of Death* and *Niagara*.

Dead Reckoning 1947

"Maybe she was all right, and maybe Christmas comes in July. But I didn't believe it."

—Humphrey Bogart (war vet Rip Murdock) about Lizabeth Scott (femme fatale Coral Chandler)

"Sometimes, chum you go soft-headed. I'd like to see any blonde do that to me."

—Humphrey Bogart (war vet Rip Murdock) to an army buddy

"It looked like feeding time at the zoo. All you needed was money to start with and bicarbonate to finish with."

—Humphrey Bogart (war vet Rip Murdock) voice-over, entering an expensive nightclub

Detour 1945

"That's life. Whichever way you turn, fate sticks out a foot to trip you."

—Tom Neal (nightclub pianist Al Roberts)

"Not only don't you have any scruples, you don't have any brains."

—Ann Savage (hitchhiker Vera) to Tom Neal (nightclub pianist Al Roberts)

"Life's like a ball game. You gotta take a swing at whatever comes along before you wake up and find it's the ninth inning."

—Ann Savage (hitchhiker Vera)

"Give a lift to a tomato, you expect her to be nice, don't you? What kinds of dames thumb rides? Sunday school teachers?"

—Edmund MacDonald (playboy Charles Haskell) to Tom Neal (nightclub pianist Al Roberts)

DARK PASSAGE 1947

"BUT I LIKE GOLDFISH. I'M GONNA GET A COUPLE FOR THE ROOM—YOU KNOW, DRESS IT UP A LITTLE BIT. IT ADDS CLASS TO THE JOINT, MAKES IT A LITTLE HOMEY."

—Tom D'Andrea (taxi driver Sam) to Humphrey Bogart (escaped con Vincent Parry)

"I WAS A SMALL-TIME CROOK UNTIL THIS VERY MINUTE, AND NOW I'M A BIG-TIME CROOK!"

—Clifton Young (blackmailer Baker)

"WHEN I GET EXCITED ABOUT SOMETHING, I GIVE IT EVERYTHING I'VE GOT. I'M FUNNY THAT WAY."

—Lauren Bacall (artist Irene Jansen) to Humphrey Bogart (escaped con Vincent Parry)

HUMPHREY **BOGART** and LAUREN **BACALL** in Warner Bros.'

DARK PASSAGE

Above: Wrongly convicted murderer Vincent Parry (Humphrey Bogart) escapes from San Quentin and is helped by artist Irene Jansen (Lauren Bacall) to obtain back-street plastic surgery to change his appearance in *Dark Passage* (1947). Directed and written by Delmer Daves from a David Goodis novel. THE TEEGARDEN/NASH COLLECTION

Double Indemnity 1944

"From the moment they met
it was murder!"
—*promotional tag-line*

"Where would the living
    room be?"
"In there, but they keep the
    liquor locked up."
"That's okay. I always carry
    my own key."
—*Fred MacMurray (insurance agent
Walter Neff) to maid*

"They say native Californians
all come from Iowa."
—*Fred MacMurray (Walter Neff)*

"And yet, Keyes, as I was
walking down the street to
the drugstore, suddenly it
came over me that everything
would go wrong. It sounds
crazy but it's true, so help
me. I couldn't hear my own
footsteps. It was the walk of a
dead man."
—*Fred MacMurray (Walter Neff)
voice-over to Edward G. Robinson
(claims investigator Barton Keyes)*

A Double Life 1948

"How's the chicken
    cacciatore?"
"It's your stomach."
—*Ronald Colman (actor Tony John)
and Shelley Winters (waitress Pat
Kroll)*

"Everybody wants to be a
detective. Must be all those
radio serials."
—*detective*

The Enforcer
aka Murder Inc. 1951

"What'd he be doing in
    church?"
"Robbin' the poor box,
    coppin' a plea. Always
    bothers me when these
    hoodlums get religion."
—*Humphrey Bogart (assistant
district attorney Martin Ferguson)
and Roy Roberts (Capt. Frank
Nelson)*

"Anything else?"

"Yeah. Burn that tent you're wearing and get yourself a suit."

—*Ted de Corsia (hired killer Joseph Rico) and Zero Mostel (small-time crook Big Babe Lazich)*

"Me? I didn't do nothin'. I didn't kill anyone. I just drove away with the body."

—*Zero Mostel (small-time crook Big Babe Lazich) to Humphrey Bogart (assistant district attorney Martin Ferguson)*

"Now I'm ready for the big stuff. Maybe even a killing."

"Never say that. A murder is a contract. A hit is the sucker that gets killed. Remember those words and use them."

—*Zero Mostel (small-time crook Big Babe Lazich) and Ted de Corsia (a hired killer Joseph Rico)*

Experiment in Terror 1962

"You've got me very well cased—isn't that the word?"

"That's the word."

—*Lee Remick (bank teller Kelly Sherwood) to Ross Martin (killer Red Lynch)*

Fallen Angel 1946

"Professor Madley's an old friend of mine."

"When was that?"

"The good old days."

"How old?"

"Old enough to be good."

—*Dana Andrews (con man Eric Stanton) and Olin Howlin (promoter Joe Ellis)*

"What a dump!"

(see the Bette Davis line in Beyond the Forest)—*Dana Andrews (con man Eric Stanton)*

Above: A drifter, Eric Stanton (Dana Andrews), is creeping around outside a diner to spy on waitress Stella (Linda Darnell), who is being ogled by her boss, "Pop" (Percy Kilbride), in the tawdry, atmospheric *Fallen Angel* (1946).

The Fallen Sparrow 1943

"Why do you want to carry
   a gun?"
"To shoot people with,
   sweetheart."
—*police inspector and John Garfield
(Spanish Civil War vet John
McKittrick)*

The Female Jungle 1955

"You don't want to interfere
   with justice, do you, Joe?"
"Justice! What you're doing
   to me is justice? I ain't
   interfering with justice,
   but you cops are
   interfering with my sleep."
—*detective and James Kodl (Joe the
bartender)*

"What you don't know won't
   hurt you."
"That's what you think."
—*James Kodl (Joe the bartender) and
Lawrence Tierney (detective Stevens)*

The File on Thelma Jordan 1950

"I'd like to say I didn't intend
to kill her, but when you
have a gun you always use it
if you have to."
—*Barbara Stanwyck (femme fatale
Thelma Jordan) to Wendell Corey
(district attorney Cleve Marshall)*

Above: Thelma Jordan
(Barbara Stanwyck), a
woman with a past, and her
dupe, assistant D.A. Cleve
Marshall (Wendell Corey) are
hunched over the dead body
of her aunt in *The File on
Thelma Jordan* (1950).
Stanwyck is the most
relentless of noir's wicked
women.

Follow Me Quietly 1949

"Follow that car!"
—*Dorothy Patrick (reporter Ann)*

"You're getting a big kick out of making me feel cheap, aren't you? Well, maybe I had it coming."
—*Dorothy Patrick (reporter Ann) to William Lundigan (detective Grant)*

"Hot case?"
"If it gets any hotter, it'll sizzle."
—*Dorothy Patrick (reporter Ann) and William Lundigan (detective Grant)*

Force of Evil 1948

"If I make you feel necessary, I'm making a mistake."
—*John Garfield (mob lawyer Joe Morse)*

"If you need a broken man to love, break your husband."
—*John Garfield (mob lawyer Joe Morse)*

42

"I wasn't strong enough to resist corruption, but I was strong enough to fight for a piece of it."

—*John Garfield (mob lawyer Joe Morse) to Beatrice Pearson (idealistic young woman Doris Lowry)*

The Gangster 1947

"Bad was what I was. I worked the rackets, dirty rackets, ugly rackets. I was no hypocrite, I knew everything I did was low and rotten. I knew what people thought of me. What difference did it make? What did I care? I got scarred, sure. You get hurt a little when you fight your way out of the gutter."

—*voice-over by Barry Sullivan (neurotic gangster Shubunka)*

Gilda 1946

"Doesn't it bother you at all that you're married?"
"Doesn't it bother you?"

—*Glenn Ford (gambler Johnny Farrell) and Rita Hayworth (his ex-lover, nightclub performer Gilda)*

"If I'd been a ranch, they would have named me the Bar Nothing."

—*Rita Hayworth (nightclub performer Gilda) to Glenn Ford (her ex-lover, gambler Johnny Farrell)*

"Statistics show there are more women in the world than anything else—except insects."

—*Glenn Ford (gambler Johnny Farrell) to Rita Hayworth (his ex-lover, nightclub performer Gilda)*

"I hated her. So I couldn't get her out of my mind for a minute. She was in the air I breathed and in the food I ate."

—*Glenn Ford (gambler Johnny Farrell) about Rita Hayworth (his ex-lover, nightclub performer Gilda)*

GILDA 1946

"I CAN NEVER GET A ZIPPER TO CLOSE. MAYBE THAT STANDS FOR SOMETHING. WHAT DO YOU THINK?"

—*Rita Hayworth (nightclub performer Gilda) to George Macready (her husband, casino owner Ballin Mundson)*

Opposite: Nightclub performer Gilda (Rita Hayworth) and gambler Johnny Farrell (Glenn Ford) go through a love-hate courtship and upset a Nazi subplot before all ends well in *Gilda* (1946). THE TEEGARDEN/ NASH COLLECTION

The Glass Key 1942

"You're slumming, and I don't go for slummers. You think you're too good for me. Well, it so happens I think I'm too good for you!"
—*Alan Ladd (Ed Beaumont) to Veronica Lake (Janet Henry)*

"I've got a little room upstairs that's too small for you to fall down in. I can bounce you around off the walls, that way we won't be wasting a lot of time while you get up off the floor."
—*William Bendix (henchman Jeff) to Alan Ladd (Ed Beaumont)*

"Here's looking at you."
"I don't want to look at you, you're a heel."
—*Alan Ladd (Ed Beaumont) and William Bendix (henchman Jeff)*

Gun Crazy
aka **Deadly Is the Female** 1950

"We go together, Laurie. I don't know why. Maybe like guns and ammunition go together."
—*John Dall (Bart Tare) to Peggy Cummins (Annie Laurie Starr)*

"You know how much it costs for two to live? Just twice as much as one."
—*meat packer to John Dall (Bart Tare)*

"You're going to see her tonight, aren't you?"
"What's wrong with that?"
"Nothin'. Only she ain't the type to make a happy home. It's just some guys are born smart about women and some are born dumb."
—*Bit player (circus clown) and John Dall (sharpshooter Bart Tare)*

THE GLASS KEY 1942

"WHAT'S THE MATTER? DON'T YOU LIKE YOUR STEAK MEDIUM?"
"WHEN I BITE A STEAK, I LIKE IT TO BITE BACK AT ME."
—*Eddie Marr (Rusty) and William Bendix (henchman Jeff)*

GUN CRAZY 1950

"WHY, WE GOT MORE WAYS OF MAKING SUCKERS THAN WE GOT SUCKERS. WHEN WE PULL OUTTA THIS BURG TOMORROW, THE NATIVES'LL HAVE NOTHING LEFT BUT SOME OLD COLLAR BUTTONS AND SOME RUSTY BOBBY PINS."
—*Bit player (circus clown) to John Dall (sharpshooter Bart Tare)*

He Walked by Night 1949

"The work of the police, like that of women, is never over."

—*voice-over narrator*

"And so the face of the unknown killer, built up from fragments of evidence, was sent out all over the country."

—*voice-over narrator*

"No one in the underworld recognized that mysterious face. He was as unknown as if he had lived in the sixteenth century."

—*voice-over narrator*

High Sierra 1941

"Look, Velma, did you ever think you'd like to go around the world?"
"Around the world? Oh, I don't know if I'd like that. It's so far. It would take so long to get back."

—*Humphrey Bogart (criminal Roy "Mad Dog" Earle) and Joan Leslie (the innocent Velma)*

"I'll never forget what happened to a guy I know, Petty Garrison. Small timer, he was. He and another hood waltzed in to heist a grocery store. They left the heap out in front with the engine running. When they come busting out a couple jumps ahead of a shotgun blast, some so-and-so had stolen it. They ducked down an alley and run into a big copper. Brother, what a mess!"

—*Arthur Kennedy (stick-up man Red Hatter)*

His Kind of Woman 1951

"I was just getting ready to take my tie off, wondering if I should hang myself with it."
—*Robert Mitchum (gambler Dan Milner) to strong-arm man*

"When I have nothing to do at night and can't think, I always iron my money."
"What do you press when you're broke?"
"When I'm broke, I press my pants."
—*Robert Mitchum (gambler Dan Milner) and Jane Russell (singer Lenore Brent)*

Opposite: The world-weary and sardonic gambler Dan Milner (Robert Mitchum) is tricked into going to Mexico so he can be murdered and his identity taken over by a deported Mafia leader. But he is saved by the voluptuous singer Lenore Brent (Jane Russell) in the dark, violent yet comic *His Kind of Woman* (1951).

'The hottest combination that ever hit the screen!'
—LOUELLA O. PARSONS

HOWARD HUGHES
presents

ROBERT MITCHUM

JANE RUSSELL

in

HIS KIND OF WOMAN.

with

VINCENT PRICE · TIM HOLT
CHARLES McGRAW

R K O
RADIO
PICTURES

A JOHN FARROW
PRODUCTION

Hollow Triumph 1948

"You're a bitter little lady."
"It's a bitter little world."
—*Paul Henreid (con man John Muller/Dr. Bartok) and Joan Bennett (secretary Evelyn Hahn)*

"I remember his haberdashery."
—*witness*

Ex-con Johnny Muller (Paul Henreid), who is on the run from the law, kills lookalike psychiatrist Dr. Victor Bartok and successfully impersonates him until his own ironic murder in the downbeat *Hollow Triumph* (1948).

Hoodlum Empire 1952

"You gotta use a little
    imagination, counsellor."
"Imagination in court is
    called perjury."
—*gangster boss and crooked tax
accountant*

"Be smart, Charlie. Act
dumb."
—*gangster boss to Forrest Tucker
(henchman Charlie Pignatelli)*

I Am a Fugitive from a Chain Gang 1932

"No friends, no rest no
    peace—keep moving,
    that's all that's left for me."
"Can't you tell me where
    you're going? Do you need
    any money? How do you
    live?"
"I steal."
—*Paul Muni (chain-gang escapee
James Allen) and Helen Vinson (his
girl Helen)*

I Wake Up Screaming 1942

"Hotcakes and coffee."
"Is that all?"
"No, but the rest of it isn't
    on the menu."
"You couldn't afford it if it
    was."
—*Allyn Joslyn (columnist Larry
Evans) and Carole Landis (waitress
Vickie Lynn)*

"I know the things I want
and I know how to get it."
—*Carole Landis (waitress Vickie
Lynn) to Betty Grable (her sister,
stenographer Jill Lynn)*

"Women are all alike."
"For pete's sake, what
    difference does that make?
    You've got to have them.
    They're standard
    equipment."
—*Alan Mowbray (actor Robin Ray)
and Allyn Joslyn (columnist Larry
Evans)*

Above: In *I Married a
Communist*, aka *The Woman
on Pier 13* (1949), Robert
Ryan plays a shipping
executive, a one-time
member of the Communist
Party, being blackmailed by
his former associates, who
want to gain a foothold in
the waterfront union.

"I'll get you eventually. If not tomorrow, next week. If not next week, next year. Time's nothing in my life. It is in yours. Each minute's an eternity to someone in your shoes."

—Laird Cregar (detective Ed Cornell) to Victor Mature (murder suspect on the run Frankie Christopher)

"We've got more wolves in New York than there are in Siberia."

—Carole Landis (waitress Vickie Lynn) to Betty Grable (her sister, stenographer Jill Lynn)

Impact 1949

"I'll never think of our moments together without nausea."

—Brian Donlevy (Walter Williams) to Helen Walker (Irene Williams)

"In this world you turn the other cheek and you get hit with a lug wrench."

—Brian Donlevy (Walter Williams)

"It's wonderful how tools seem to come alive in your hands!"

—Ella Raines (garage owner Helen Walker) to Brian Donlevy (Walter Williams)

Opposite: Lady's maid Su Lin (Anna May Wong) tells her father that her employer's husband, Walter Williams (Brian Donlevy), is a wanted man, in *Impact* (1949).

Above: The body on the side of the hill is that of a would-be murderer. His intended victim was his lover's husband, Walter Williams (Brian Donlevy), who escapes, but in an ironic twist becomes wanted for murder himself in *Impact*.

In a Lonely Place 1950

"It was his story against mine, but of course I told my story better."

—*Humphrey Bogart (screenwriter Dix Steele)*

"Do you look down on all women? Or just the ones you know."

—*Gloria Grahame (Laurel Gray) to Humphrey Bogart (her lover screenwriter Dix Steele)*

"I said I liked it, I didn't say I wanted to kiss it."

—*Gloria Grahame (Laurel Gray) to Humphrey Bogart (her lover screenwriter Dix Steele)*

"I was born when you kissed me. I died when you left me. I lived a few weeks while you loved me."

—*Humphrey Bogart (scriptwriter Dix Steele) quoted by Gloria Grahame (his lover Laurel Gray)*

Journey into Fear 1943

"You're a ballistics expert, and you've never fired a gun?"
"Well, I just never did."
"It's very simple—you just point it and pull the trigger."

—*Everett Sloane (arms salesman Kopeikin) and Joseph Cotten (armament engineer Howard Graham)*

The Killers 1946

"What's the idea?"
"There isn't any idea."

—*Phil Brown (Nick) to Charles McGraw (killer Al)*

"I did something wrong— once."

—*Burt Lancaster (Ole "Swede" Anderson)*

"Will he be able to talk anymore?"
"He's dead now, except he's breathing."

—*Edmond O'Brien (insurance investigator Riordan) and doctor*

KEY LARGO 1948

"GEE, HONEY, YOU'RE AS MEAN AS CAN BE."

—*Claire Trevor (gangster moll Gaye Dawn) to Edward G. Robinson (gangster Johnny Rocco)*

"IT'S BETTER TO BE A LIVE COWARD THAN A DEAD HERO."

—*Claire Trevor (gangster moll Gaye Dawn) to Humphrey Bogart (war vet Frank McCloud)*

"IF I'D KNOWN YOU WAS GONNA ACT THIS WAY, I NEVER WOULD HAVE COME HERE!"
"IF I'D KNOWN WHAT YOU WERE LIKE, YOU WOULDN'T HAVE BEEN ASKED."

—*Claire Trevor (gangster moll Gaye Dawn) and Edward G. Robinson (gangster Johnny Rocco)*

Above: Naval engineer Howard Graham (Joseph Cotten) gets caught up in dangerous foreign intrigue and tries to discover how much the stripper Josette (Dolores Del Rio) knows about who's trying to kill him. *Journey into Fear* (1942) was directed by Norman Foster (and by an uncredited Orson Welles, who also appears in the film).

The Killing 1956

"I know you like a book, ya little tramp. You'd sell out your own mother for a piece of fudge. But you're smart with it. Smart enough to know when to sell and when to sit tight. You've got a great big dollar sign there where most women have a heart."
—*Sterling Hayden (ex-con Johnny Clay) to Marie Windsor (gold-digger Sherry Peatty)*

Kiss Me, Deadly 1955

"What's the matter? Were you out with a guy who thought no was a three-letter word?"
—*Ralph Meeker (private eye Mike Hammer) to Cloris Leachman (hitchhiker Christina Bailey)*

"He's a bedroom dick."
—*policeman*

"You're never around when I need you."
"You never need me when I'm around."
—*Maxine Cooper (secretary Velda) and Ralph Meeker (her boss, private eye Mike Hammer)*

Kiss of Death 1947

"I wouldn't give ya the skin off a grape!"
—*Richard Widmark (killer Tommy Udo)*

Opposite: In *Kansas City Confidential* (1952), ex-con Joe Rolfe's (John Payne) search for the hoods who framed him takes him to Mexico, where one of the real robbers, Tony (Lee Van Cleef), tries to strongarm him while the mastermind, Timothy Foster (Preston Foster), looks on.

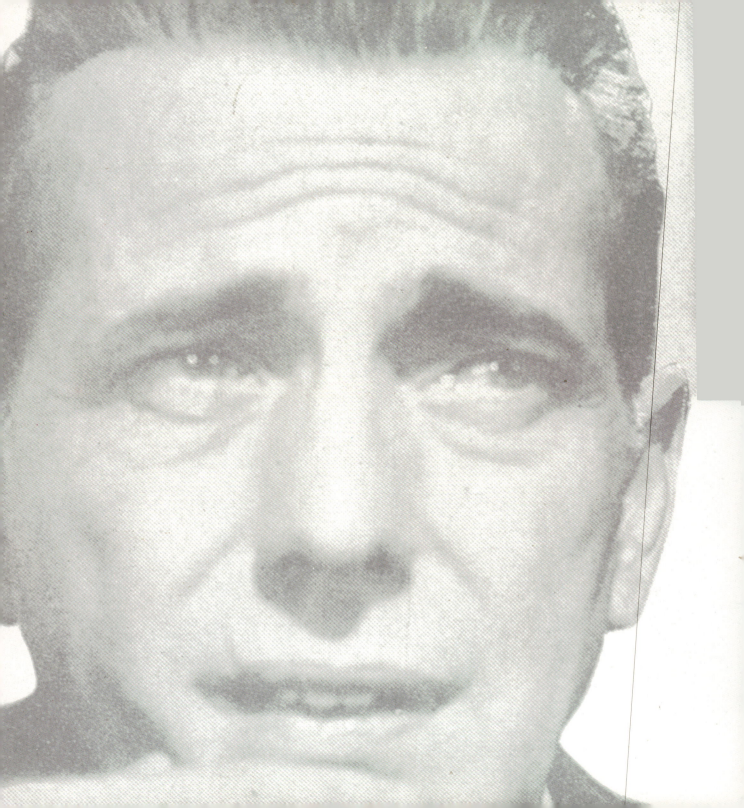

Knock on Any Door 1949

"Live fast, die young and have
a good-looking corpse."

—John Derek (petty criminal Nick
"Pretty Boy" Romano)

"Did I ask to be born? Did I?"

—John Derek (petty criminal Nick
"Pretty Boy" Romano)

"I hope it works out."

"So do I, but there've been
  very few miracles since
  the thirteenth century."

"Oh, if I were as cynical as
  you, I'd hang myself."

"I'd be too cynical to trust
  the rope."

—social worker and Humphrey

Bogart (lawyer Andrew Morton)

Top: Juvenile delinquent Nick
Romano (John Derek) lurks
in the shadows, knife at the
ready, while a cop (bit
player) looks the wrong way
in Nicholas Ray's *Knock on
Any Door* (1949). This film
was John Derek's film debut.

Opposite: Humphrey Bogart
in a detail from a magazine
advertisement for *Knock on
Any Door*.

Lady from Shanghai 1948

"I don't have to listen to
    you talk like that."
"Oh yes you do, lover."

—*Everett Sloane (crippled lawyer
Arthur Bannister) to Rita Hayworth
(his wife, femme fatale Elsa Bannister)*

Lady in the Lake 1947

"I don't like your manner."
"I'm not selling it."

—*Audrey Trotter (crime reporter
Adrienne Fromsett) and Robert
Montgomery (private eye Philip
Marlowe)*

Laura 1944

"It's lavish, but I call it home."

—*Clifton Webb (radio personality
Waldo Lydecker) to Dana Andrews
(detective Mark McPherson)*

"I ain't afraid of cops. I was
brought up to spit whenever
I saw one."

—*maid*

"McPherson, tell me, why
    did they have to
    photograph her in that
    horrible condition?"
"When a dame gets killed,
    she doesn't care about how
    she looks."
"Will you stop calling her a
    dame? Look around. Is
    this the home of a dame?"

—*Clifton Webb (radio personality
Waldo Lydecker) and Dana Andrews
(detective Mark McPherson)*

"Murder is my favorite
crime."

—*Clifton Webb (radio personality
Waldo Lydecker) to Dana Andrews
(detective Mark McPherson)*

"I don't use a pen. I write
with a goose quill dipped in
venom."

—*Clifton Webb (radio personality
Waldo Lydecker)*

Opposite: Bette Davis as
Leslie Crosbie, a woman who
shoots the man she loves in a
jealous rage. She beats the
rap but later dies (to satisfy
the Production Code
requirement of the time that
murderers must be
punished) in a tropical noir,
The Letter (1940).

BETTE DAVIS

THE LETTER

Country of Origin U. S. A.

"I STILL LOVE THE MAN I KILLED." —*Bette Davis (Leslie Crosbie)*

The Lost Weekend 1945

"Don Birnam is dead already.
   He died over this
   weekend."
"Did he? What did he die of?"
"Of a lot of things—of
   alcohol, of moral anemia,
   of fear, shame, DTs."
*—Ray Milland (alcoholic writer
Don Birnam) and Jane Wyman (his
girlfriend Helen St. James)*

"Most men lead lives of quiet
desperation. I can't take quiet
desperation."
*—Ray Milland (alcoholic writer
Don Birnam)*

Macao 1952

"Some girls don't think I'm
   so bad."
"It's all a matter of taste."
*—Robert Mitchum (war vet
Nick Cochran) and Jane Russell
(nightclub singer Julie Benton)*

The Maltese Falcon 1941

"I distrust a close-mouthed
man. He generally picks the
wrong time to talk and says
the wrong things. Talking is
something you can't do
judiciously unless you keep
in practice."
*—Sydney Greenstreet (suspicious
character Casper "Fat Man"
Gutman) to Humphrey Bogart
(private eye Sam Spade)*

"Don't be sure I'm as crooked
as I'm supposed to be."
*—Humphrey Bogart (private eye Sam
Spade)*

"When you're slapped, you'll
take it and like it."
*—Humphrey Bogart (private eye Sam
Spade)*

Opposite: Ex-G.I. Nick Cochrane (Robert Mitchum) stands in the hallway of a seedy hotel, waiting for the expected attack from a hired thug in *Macao* (1952), directed separately by both Nicholas Ray and Josef von Sternberg (though only Sternberg is credited). The film features the song "You Kill Me."

The Manchurian Candidate 1962

"Oh, Raymond, what is the matter with you? You look as if your head were going to grow to a point in the next thirteen seconds."
—*Angela Lansbury (ambitious Mrs. Iselin) to Laurence Harvey (her son Raymond Shaw)*

"The twelve days of Christmas! One day of Christmas is horrible enough."
—*Laurence Harvey (Raymond Shaw) to Frank Sinatra (Bennett Marco)*

"It's a terrible thing to hate your mother. But I didn't always hate her. When I was a child, I only kind of disliked her."
—*Laurence Harvey (Raymond Shaw) to Frank Sinatra (Bennett Marco)*

Marked Woman 1937

"All my dresses are beautiful. They gotta be in this racket. There's nothin' like clothes, that's the sugar makes the flies come round."
—*Isabel Jewell (clip-joint hostess Emmy Lou) to Jane Bryan (Betty)*

"I'll get even if I have to crawl back from the grave."
—*Bette Davis (Mary Dwight) to Eduardo Ciannelli (gangster Johnny Vanning)*

"You know, the law isn't for people like us."
"What is?"
"Well, that's another thing I've been trying to figure out for years."
—*Lola Lane (clip-joint hostess Gaby) to Bette Davis (clip-joint hostess Mary Dwight)*

Opposite: Nightclub girl Mary Dwight (Bette Davis) testifies against the gangster who killed her kid sister, but is scarred for life by him in revenge. *Marked Woman* (1937) is a pre-noir noted for its trailblazing depiction of women fighting for their rights, or as star Bette Davis said: "At last a part I can get my teeth into." THE TEEGARDEN/ NASH COLLECTION

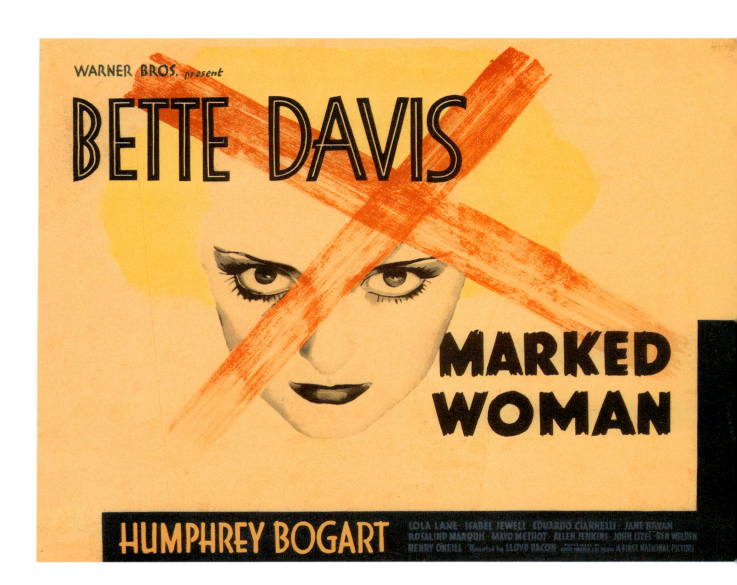

Mildred Pierce 1945

"Know that guy?"
"Yes, we were married once."
—*waitress and Joan Crawford (self-made businesswoman Mildred Pierce)*

"Personally, I'm convinced that alligators have the right idea. They eat their young."
—*Eve Arden (Ida)*

"I was always in the kitchen. I felt as though I'd been born in a kitchen and lived there all my life except for the few hours it took to get married."
—*Joan Crawford (self-made businesswoman Mildred Pierce) voice-over*

"Friendship's a lot more lasting than love."
"Yeah, but not as entertaining."
—*Joan Crawford (self-made businesswoman Mildred Pierce) and Jack Carson (her business partner Wally Fay)*

MILDRED PIERCE 1945

"I LOVE YOU TOO, MOTHER, BUT LET'S NOT GET STICKY ABOUT IT."
—*Anne Blyth (spoiled Veda Pierce) to Joan Crawford (her mother Mildred Pierce)*

Opposite: Businesswoman Mildred Pierce (Joan Crawford) tries to save her wayward daughter Veda (Ann Blyth) by confessing to the murder the youngster committed in *Mildred Pierce* (1945), based on a novel by the noir master James M. Cain. THE TEEGARDEN/NASH COLLECTION

JOAN **CRAWFORD**

JACK **CARSON**

ZACHARY **SCOTT**

Mil

red **Pierce** WARNER BROS.

Moonrise 1949

"Sure is remarkable how
dying can make a saint of a
man."

—*Allyn Joslyn (sheriff Clem Otis) to
his wife about a dead bully*

"Educated fellow, that Mose.
  Engineer says he can read
  as good as anybody."
"Better. Read about every
  book there is, I guess."
"That's too many."

—*Allyn Joslyn (sheriff Clem Otis)
and Dane Clark (murderer's son
Danny Hawkins) about a black
caretaker*

Murder, My Sweet 1944

"She was a charming middle-aged lady with a face like a bucket of mud. I gave her a drink. She was a gal who'd take a drink if she had to knock you down to get the bottle."
—*Dick Powell (private eye Philip Marlowe) voice-over*

"You know, this'll be the first time I've ever killed anyone I knew so little and liked so well."
—*Claire Trevor (femme fatale Mrs. Grayle/Velma) to Dick Powell (private eye Philip Marlowe)*

"She was cute as lace pants."
—*Mike Mazurki (ex-con Moose Malloy) about Claire Trevor (his girlfriend Velma)*

"I felt pretty good—like an amputated leg."
—*Dick Powell (private eye Philip Marlowe)*

"If I always knew what I meant, I'd be a genius."
—*Dick Powell (private eye Philip Marlowe)*

My Gun Is Quick 1957

"I just crawled out of a sewer. There's not a decent person left in this world."
—*Robert Bray (private eye Mike Hammer) to his secretary*

"A nice kid was murdered. You know that fries me, Pat."
—*Robert Bray (private eye Mike Hammer) to his secretary*

The Naked City 1948

"Ever try to catch a murderer? It has its depressing moments."
—*voice-over narrator*

THE NAKED KISS 1964

"I SAW A BROKEN-DOWN PIECE OF MACHINERY. NOTHING BUT THE BUCK, THE BED AND THE BOTTLE FOR THE REST OF MY LIFE. THAT'S WHAT I SAW."
—*Constance Towers (prostitute Kelly)*

Opposite: Prostitute Kelly (Constance Towers), bald sans wig, decides to go straight. After knocking out her pimp, she is taking back her earnings, in Sam Fuller's notorious *The Naked Kiss* (1964).

67

Opposite: Pampered playboy
and murderer Frank Niles
(Howard Duff) in director
Jules Dassin's docu-style *The
Naked City* (1948), which
won cinematographer
William Daniels an Academy
Award and became a popular
TV series in the 1950s.

NED CITY

STARRING BARR
FITZGERAL

dca
RE-RELEASE

2

The Narrow Margin 1952

"You make me sick to my
   stomach!"
"Yeah? Well use your own
   sink."
—*Charles McGraw (detective Walter
Brown) and Marie Windsor
(racketeer's widow Mrs. Neil)*

"What kind of a dish was
she? The sixty-cent special—
cheap, flashy, strictly poison
under the gravy."
—*Charles McGraw (detective Walter
Brown) about Marie Windsor
(racketeer's widow Mrs. Neil)*

Niagara 1953

"Niagara and Marilyn Monroe
—the two most electrifying
sights in the world."
—*trailer*

"Sure I'm meeting somebody.
Just anybody handy as long
as he's a man."
—*Marilyn Monroe (faithless wife
Rose Loomis)*

Night and the City 1950

"You're very sharp, Mr.
Fabian. You've done a very
sharp thing, maybe even
sharp enough to cut your
throat."
—*Herbert Lom (wrestling promoter
Kristo) to Richard Widmark (clip-
joint tout and aspiring wrestling
promoter Harry Fabian)*

Night of the Hunter 1955

"Well, now, what's it to be,
Lord? Another widow? How
many has it been—six?
Twelve? I disremember. You
say the word and I'm on my
way."
—*Robert Mitchum (psychotic
killer/preacher Harry Powell)
thinking aloud*

No Way Out 1950

"I used to live in a sewer. Now I live in a swamp. I've come up in the world."
—*Linda Darnell (embittered white trash)*

Nocturne 1946

"Don't your nose get sore, sticking it all the time in other people's business?"
—*Myrna Dell (maid Susan Flanders) to George Raft (Lt. Joe Warne)*

"You through wasting the city's film, Olson?"
"Why can't a pretty girl bump herself once? Gets monotonous taking pictures of men all the time."
—*Walter Sande (Lt. Halberson) and William Challee (police photographer)*

"You're gonna have a hard time holding me."
"Be fun trying."
—*Myrna Dell (maid Susan Flanders) and Walter Sande (Lt. Halberson)*

"You never can depend on girls named Dolores."
—*George Raft (Lt. Joe Warne)*

"He was a ladykiller. But don't get any ideas—I ain't no lady."
—*Myrna Dell (maid Susan Flanders) to police*

NOTORIOUS 1946

"WHY DO YOU LIKE THAT SONG?"
**"BECAUSE IT'S A LOT OF HOOEY.
THERE'S NOTHING LIKE A LOVE
SONG TO GIVE YOU A GOOD
LAUGH."**
—*Cary Grant (federal agent Devlin) and*
Ingrid Bergman (playgirl Alicia Huberman)

"DON'T YOU NEED A COAT?"
"YOU'LL DO."
—*Cary Grant (federal agent Devlin) and*
Ingrid Bergman (playgirl Alicia Huberman)

Opposite: Federal agent
Devlin (Cary Grant) and
Alicia Huberman (Ingrid
Bergman), playgirl daughter
of a Nazi agent, work
together in Rio de Janeiro to
entrap Nazi conspirator
Alexander Sebastian (Claude
Rains) on far right and his
mother (Mme Konstantin) in
Alfred Hitchcock's *Notorious*
(1946). THE TEEGARDEN/NASH
COLLECTION

72

Out of the Past 1947

"That isn't the way to play
  it."
"Why not?"
" 'Cause it isn't the way to
  win."
"Is there a way to win?"
"Well, there's a way to lose
  more slowly."
—*Robert Mitchum (private eye
Jeff Bailey) and Jane Greer
(racketeer's girl Kathie Moffett)*

"I never saw her in the
daytime. We seemed to live
by night. What was left of
the day went away like a
pack of cigarettes you
smoked."
—*Robert Mitchum (private eye
Jeff Bailey) voice-over*

"Two things I can smell
inside a hundred feet.
Burning hamburger and a
romance."
—*bit player*

"You're like a leaf that the
wind blows from one gutter
to another."
—*Robert Mitchum (private eye Jeff
Bailey) to Jane Greer (racketeer's girl
Kathie Moffett)*

Panic in the Streets 1950

"You know, my mother
  always told me if you look
  deep enough in anybody
  you'd always find some
  good, but I don't know
  about you."
"With apologies to your
  mother, that's the second
  mistake she made."
—*Richard Widmark (Dr. Clint
Reid) and Paul Douglas (Captain
Warren)*

"If there's anything I don't
like, it's a smart-cracking
dame."
—*Jack Palance (small-time crook
Blackie)*

ON DANGEROUS GROUND 1951

"SERVE DRINKS TO JUVENILES,
  YOU'LL GET INTO TROUBLE.
  HOW MANY TIMES DO I
  HAVE TO TELL YOU THAT?"
"WHAT DO YA WANT ME TO DO?
  EVERY DAME THAT COMES IN
  HERE, LOOK AT HER TEETH?"
—*Robert Ryan (Detective Jim Wilson)
and bartender*

"MAKE UP YOUR MIND TO BE A
COP—NOT A GANGSTER WITH A
BADGE."
—*Ed Begley (Captain Brawley) to Robert Ryan
(Detective Jim Wilson)*

The Paradine Case 1947

"I will tell you about Mrs. Paradine. She's bad. Bad to the bone."

—*Louis Jourdan (valet Andre Latour) to Gregory Peck (barrister Anthony Keene)*

"Men who've been good too long get a longing for the mud and want to wallow in it."

—*lawyer's daughter about Gregory Peck (barrister Anthony Keene)*

Party Girl 1958

"Self-destruction among showgirls seems to be a kind of occupational hazard. Probably the cheery atmosphere of nightclub life."

—*Robert Taylor (crippled mob lawyer Thomas Farrell) to Cyd Charisse (showgirl Vickie Gaye)*

"I'll handle your business for you, Rico. I'll even protect your hoods for you, but I refuse to eat with you, because you're a slob."

—*Robert Taylor (crippled mob lawyer Thomas Farrell) to Lee J. Cobb (mob boss Rico Angelo)*

The Petrified Forest 1936

"It looks like I'll spend the rest of my life dead."

—*Humphrey Bogart (killer Duke Mantee)*

"You can't tell a killer except by his chin. There's a funny thing about that. A killer always holds his chin in."

—*Charley Grapewin (Granpa Maple)*

THE PETRIFIED FOREST 1936

"IF YOU'LL TAKE MY ADVICE, SON—I WOULDN'T START ANY SHOOTING IN THAT GET-UP."
"WHY NOT?"
"I'VE NEVER SEEN A BETTER TARGET."

—*Charley Grapewin (Granpa Maple) and Porter Hale (would-be vigilante Jason Maple)*

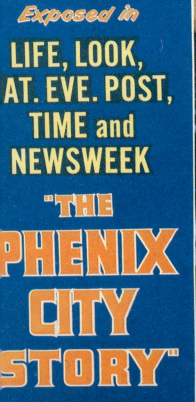

Exposed in

LIFE, LOOK,
AT. EVE. POST,
TIME and
NEWSWEEK

"THE
PHENIX
CITY
STORY"

starring

n McINTIRE · Richard KILEY · Kathryn GRANT
Edward ANDREWS · Meg MYLES · James EDWARDS
duced by Samuel BISCHOFF & David DIAMOND
Directed by Phil KARLSON · Screenplay by
Crane WILBUR and Daniel MAINWARING
AN ALLIED ARTISTS Picture

Phantom Lady 1944

"You like jive?"
"You bet. I'm a hep kitten."
—*Elisha Cook, Jr. (drummer Cliff March) and Ella Raines (sleuthing secretary Carol "Kansas" Richman)*

"No names, no addresses. Just companions for the evening."
—*Fay Helm (Ann Terry, "the Phantom Lady") to Alan Curtis (engineer Scott Henderson)*

"What a place. I can feel the rats in the wall."
—*Franchot Tone (sculptor Jack Marlow) to Elisha Cook, Jr. (drummer Cliff March)*

Pickup on South Street 1953

"Do you know what Communism is?"
"Who cares?"
—*Federal agent and Richard Widmark (pickpocket Skip McCoy)*

"He's as shifty as smoke, but I love him."
—*Thelma Ritter (police informer Moe)*

"Every extra buck has a meaning all its own."
—*Thelma Ritter (police informer Moe)*

"All right, muffin, let's have a dose of straight talk."
—*Thelma Ritter (police informer Moe) to Jean Peters (spy's ex-girl Candy)*

"You'll always be a two-bit cannon, and when they pick you up in the gutter dead, your hand'll be in a drunk's pocket."
—*Murvyn Vye (Capt. Dan Tiger) to Richard Widmark (pickpocket Skip McCoy)*

Opposite: For over one hundred years Phenix City, Alabama, was notorious for violence and lawlessness. Director Phil Karlson's documentary/exposé style noir, called *The Phenix City Story* (1955), is a recreation of the events leading up to the big clean-up of the town.

Pitfall 1948

"You're the strangest husband I ever had."
—*Jane Wyatt (Sue Forbes) to Dick Powell (her husband John)*

"Have you ever noticed if for some reason you want to feel completely out of step with the rest of the world, the only thing to do is sit around a cocktail lounge in the afternoon?"
—*Lizabeth Scott (model Mona Stevens) to Dick Powell (insurance agent Johnny Forbes)*

"I bet you never thought of
    me as a man who could
    fall in love."
"You'd be surprised how little
    time I have to think about
    you at all, Mac."
—*Raymond Burr (private eye MacDonald) and Dick Powell (insurance agent Johnny Forbes)*

Right: Insurance agent gone bad John Forbes (Dick Powell) ponders the existential prison of his suburban life in André de Toth's *Pitfall* (1948).

Above: Dick Powell plays a happily married man who gets mixed up with murder while under the spell of femme fatale Lizabeth Scott in *Pitfall*.

A Place in the Sun 1951

"I see you had a misspent youth."

—*Elizabeth Taylor (rich girl Angela Vickers) to Montgomery Clift (ambitious George Eastman)*

"You seem so strange. So deep and far away. As though you were holding something back."
"I am."
"Don't."

—*Elizabeth Taylor (Angela Vickers) and Montgomery Clift (George Eastman)*

Plunder Road 1957

"Too bad my wife couldn't hold out. She waited for me for twenty-three years while I'm in and out of stir like it was a revolving door. Two months ago, she dies."

—*Elisha Cook, Jr. (petty criminal Skeets) to Wayne Morris (fellow criminal Commando) as they're driving away from a train robbery*

"No wonder you got sent up so many times—you think cops are dumb."

—*Wayne Morris (Commando) to Elisha Cook, Jr. (train robber Skeets)*

Above: Petty crook and loser Skeets (Elisha Cook, Jr.) holds onto the TNT that is going to help his ill-fated gang steal a trainload of gold bullion in director Hubert Cornfield's *Plunder Road* (1957).

The Postman Always Rings Twice 1946

"Well, so long, mister. Thanks for the ride, the three cigarettes and for not laughing at my theories on life."

—*John Garfield (drifter Frank Chambers)*

"He used to be a dick, but he's not a dick any more. He works for me. He's a gumshoe man."

—*Hume Cronyn (Arthur Keats)*

"Blind man without a cane could see you're in a bad way."

—*Hume Cronyn (Arthur Keats) to John Garfield (drifter Frank Chambers)*

"With my brains and your looks, we could go places."

—*John Garfield (drifter Frank Chambers) to Audrey Trotter (Madge Gorland)*

The Prowler 1951

"You don't like being a policeman, do you?"
"Why should I?"
"Well, for one thing, you look nice in a uniform."

—*Evelyn Keyes (Susan Gilvray) and Van Heflin (bad cop Webb Garwood)*

"You murdered my husband. You would have killed the doctor."
"So what? So I'm no good. But I'm no worse than anybody else."

—*Evelyn Keyes (Susan Gilvray) and Van Heflin (bad cop Webb Garwood)*

"You work in a store, you knock down the cash register. A big boss, the income tax. A ward heeler, you sell votes. A lawyer, take bribes. I was a cop, I used a gun. But whatever I did, I did for you."

—*Van Heflin (bad cop Webb Garwood) to Evelyn Keyes (Susan Gilvray)*

PUSHOVER 1957

"MONEY'S NICE, BUT IT DOESN'T MAKE THE WORLD GO ROUND."
"DON'T IT?"

—*Phil Carey (detective Rick McAllister) and Fred MacMurray (detective Paul Sheridan)*

"MONEY ISN'T DIRTY, JUST PEOPLE."

—*Kim Novak (ex-gangster moll Leona McLane)*

The Racket 1951

"How do you think I got where I did? Not by being outsmarted by clucks like you."
—*Robert Ryan (mobster Nick Scanlon) to a group of thugs*

Raw Deal 1948

"I told you he had a cash register mind. Rings every time he opens his mouth."
—*Dennis O'Keefe (escaped convict Joe Sullivan) to Marsha Hunt (hostage Ann Martin).*

Riffraff 1947

"Where are you from?"
"Oh, here, there, and everywhere."
"That's a beautiful country, that everywhere."
—*Pat O'Brien (private eye Dan Hammer), Anne Jeffreys (chanteuse Maxine) and Percy Kilbride (taxi driver Pops)*

Road House 1948

"Have a drink. I kept the bar open for you."
"Sure, I could use a little cooking sherry."
—*Richard Widmark (roadhouse owner Jefty) and Ida Lupino (singer Lily Stevens)*

"She reminds me of the first woman who ever slapped my face."
—*man in bar about Ida Lupino (singer Lily Stevens)*

"Doesn't it ever enter a man's head that a woman can do without him?"
—*Ida Lupino (singer Lily Stevens) to Cornel Wilde (roadhouse manager Pete Morgan)*

THE RACKET 1951

"I HEAR YOU'RE LIVING IN THE SAME OLD DUMP."
"HOUSE IS WHAT IT'S CALLED."
—*Robert Ryan (Nick Scanlon) and Robert Mitchum (Captain McQuigg)*

"BLOW, SHYSTER."
—*Robert Ryan (Nick Scanlon)*

Opposite: Mobster Nick Scanlon (Robert Ryan) with his moll Irene (the sexy-voiced Lizabeth Scott), who sings "A Lovely Way to Spend an Evening" shortly before spending the night in jail in *The Racket* (1951).

WHO PAYS OFF WHO ..AND WHY!

HOWARD HUGHES presents

THE RACKET

starring

ROBERT MITCHUM · LIZABETH SCOTT · ROBERT RYAN

an EDMUND GRAINGER production

Directed by
JOHN CROMWELL

Screen play by
WILLIAM WISTER HAINES
and W. R. BURNETT

RKO RADIO

83

Scarlet Street 1945

"I've wanted to laugh in your face ever since I first met you. You're old, ugly and I'm sick of you—sick, sick, sick."

—Joan Bennett (femme fatale Kitty March) to Edward G. Robinson (her sugar daddy Chris Cross)

"You wouldn't know love if
    it hit you in the face."
"If that's where it hits you—
    you ought to know."

—Joan Bennett (femme fatale Kitty March) and Margaret Lindsay (Millie)

"Oh, I wouldn't think of letting you go out alone, darling. You might get run over by a streetcar."

—Dan Duryea (con man Johnny Prince) to Margaret Lindsay (Millie)

"Who do you think you are,
    my guardian angel?"
"I lost my wings a long time
    ago."

—Joan Bennett (Kitty March) and Margaret Lindsay (Millie)

84

Opposite: Femme fatale Kitty March (Joan Bennett) proves irresistible to her victim, Christopher Cross (Edward G. Robinson), a meek bank teller and amateur painter in Fritz Lang's classic *Scarlet Street* (1945).

Right: Edward G. Robinson in a detail from a magazine advertisement for *Scarlet Street*.

The Second Woman 1950

"How did you get past the NO VISITORS sign?"
"I walked straight past it."
—*Robert Young (architect Jeff Cohalan) and Betsy Drake (his girlfriend Ellen Foster)*

Shadow of a Doubt 1943

"If I wanted to murder you tomorrow, I'd find out if you were alone, walk in, hit you on the head with a lead pipe or a loaded cane—"
"What would be the fun of that? Where's your planning?"
—*Henry Travers (Joseph Newton) and Hume Cronyn (Herbie Hawkins)*

"There's one good thing in being a widow, isn't there? You don't have to ask your husband for money."
—*Frances Carson (widow Mrs. Poetter) to Joseph Cotten (murderer Uncle Charlie)*

"Do you know the world is a foul sty? Do you know if you ripped the fronts off houses you'd find swine? The world's a hell."
—*Joseph Cotten (murderer Uncle Charlie) to Teresa Wright (his niece, nicknamed Charlie)*

Shanghai Express 1932

"It took more than one man to change my name to Shanghai Lily."
—*Marlene Dietrich (femme fatale Shanghai Lily)*

The Shanghai Gesture 1941

"What a witches' sabbath . . . so incredibly evil. I didn't think such a place existed except in my own imagination—like a half-remembered dream. Anything could happen here, at any moment."
—*Gene Tierney (gambler Poppy)*

Above: Doctor Omar (Victor Mature) and B girl Dixie Pomeroy (Phyllis Brooks) in the delirious noir world of Josef von Sternberg's *The Shanghai Gesture* (1941), which he claims to have directed from his sick bed.

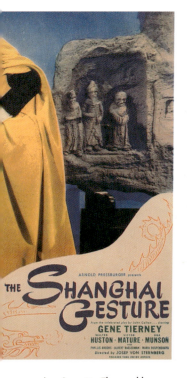

Opposite: The gambler
known only as Poppy
(Gene Tierney) poses in
Mother Gin Sling's casino,
her second home, in *The
Shanghai Gesture*. THE

TEEGARDEN/NASH COLLECTION

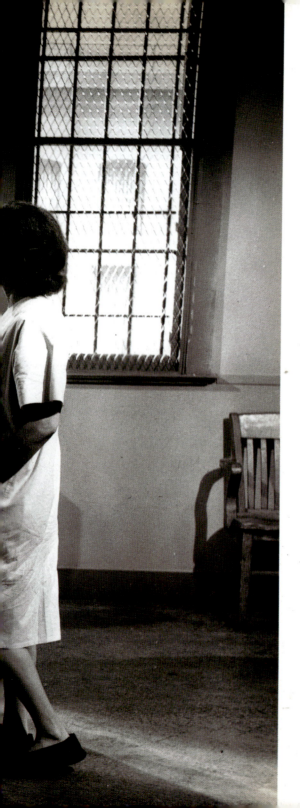

Shock Corridor 1963

"Get off it! You're in a hopped-up show-off stage. Don't be Moses leading your lunatics to the Pulitzer Prize."

—Constance Towers (stripper Kathy) to Peter Breck (reporter Johnny)

"My yen for you goes up and down like a fever chart."

—Peter Breck (reporter Johnny) to Constance Towers (stripper Kathy) during fantasy sequence

Singapore 1947

"I like troubled times. They keep the police occupied."

—Thomas Gomez (gangster Mr. Mauribus) to Fred MacMurray (pearl smuggler Matthew Gordon)

"I was always sorry the war interrupted our relationship. It promised to be delightful."

—Richard Hayden (Deputy Commissioner Hewitt) to Fred MacMurray (Matthew Gordon)

Opposite: Reporter Johnny (Peter Breck), who has checked into a mental asylum to investigate a murder, is trapped by a menacing group of women in *Shock Corridor* (1963), described in publicity material as "a journey into a medical jungle doctors won't talk about."

Slaughter on Tenth Avenue 1957

"Cockeye Cook did it, him and two of his meatballs."
—*dying murder victim*

"Little guys. All my life, I hated little guys. One day I'm gonna pull his tongue out."
—*midget*

Sleep, My Love 1948

"You like pearls, don't you."
"Don't you?"
"As a matter of fact, I sort of
    hate to think of itchy oysters
    going to all that trouble."
—*Robert Cummings (Bruce Elcott) and Claudette Colbert (Alison Courtland)*

"We've got a lot—but we haven't got everything. I want what she's got. All of it. I want her house, her name, her man. And I want them now. Tonight."
—*Hazel Brooks (model Daphne) to Don Ameche (her lover Richard Courtland)*

Sorry, Wrong Number 1948

"What does a dame like you want with a guy like me?"
—*Burt Lancaster (Henry Stevenson) to Barbara Stanwyck (his wife-to-be Leona)*

Spellbound 1945

"I have no memory. It's like looking into a mirror and seeing nothing but the mirror."
—*Gregory Peck (Dr. Anthony Edwardes) to Ingrid Bergman (Dr. Constance Peterson)*

"I'm from Pittsburgh. There's a town for you. You really can meet people in Pittsburgh. Friendly. A fellow could live and die in this town and he couldn't meet nobody."
—*businessman to Ingrid Bergman (Dr. Constance Peterson)*

Opposite: Alison Courtland (Claudette Colbert) clutches Bruce Elcott (Robert Cummings), as they are menaced by the shadow of death; her husband is trying to drive her to suicide so that he can inherit her wealth in Douglas Sirk's nightmarish *Sleep, My Love* (1948).

"Good night, Dr. Brueloff, and thanks for everything."
"Any husband of Constance's is a husband of mine."

—*Gregory Peck (Dr. Anthony Edwardes) and Michael Checkhov (Dr. Alex Brueloff)*

The Spiral Staircase 1945

"Where's my brandy?"
"I finished it for your own good."

—*Rhys Williams (manservant Oates) and Elsa Lanchester (cook Emma)*

"There is no room for imperfection in this world . . . What a pity my father didn't live to see me strong, to dispose of the weak of the world whom he detested. He would have admired me for what I am going to do."

—*George Brent (killer Professor Parry)*

"Men like to see women cry. It makes them feel superior."

—*George Brent (Professor Parry)*

The Steel Trap 1952

"The difference between the honest and the dishonest is a debatable line. We're suckers if we don't try to cram as much happiness as possible in our brief time, no matter how. Everybody breaks the law."

—*Joseph Cotten (banker)*

Opposite: Directed by, produced by, and starring actor Cornel Wilde, *Storm Fear* (1955) follows Wilde as a criminal gang leader on the lam who seeks refuge with his brother's unwilling family.

THE STRANGER
1946

"KNEW DAMN WELL IT
WAS THE SAME FELLER.
COURSE HE'S CHANGED
SOME. BEING BURIED IN
THE EARTH DOES THAT."
—*drugstore owner*

Opposite: Government agent Wilson (Edward G. Robinson) trails war criminal Franz Kindler (Orson Welles) to a small town and saves socialite Mary Longstreet (Loretta Young) from a fate worse than death in the perverse and surreal *The Stranger* (1946).

THE TEEGARDEN/NASH COLLECTION

EDWARD G. ROBIN

INTERNATIONAL PICTURES
presentation of

ON · LORETTA YOUNG · ORSON WELLES

Stranger

RELEASED THROUGH RKO RADIO PICTURES

The Strange Love of Martha Ivers

1946

"Couldn't you see
    blackmail in his eyes?"
"I haven't your experience
    with criminals."
—*Kirk Douglas (district attorney*
Walter O'Neil) and Barbara
Stanwyck (his wife Martha Ivers)

"You don't seem very sorry."
"I am sorry. Sorry that I was
    caught."
—*Judith Anderson (Mrs. Ivers) and*
Barbara Stanwyck (Martha Ivers)

"What happened?"
"Small accident. The road
    curved but I didn't."
—*sailor and Van Heflin (Sam*
Masterson)

Opposite: The cruel and
obsessive Martha Ivers
(Barbara Stanwyck) looks on
disdainfully as an old friend,
Sam Masterson (Van Heflin),
ministers to her drunken
husband and murder
accomplice Walter (Kirk
Douglas) in *The Strange Love
of Martha Ivers* (1946).

Stranger on the Third Floor 1940

"It wasn't very nice. His throat was cut. Blood was still dripping into the open drawer of the cash register."

—*Elisha Cook, Jr. (accused murderer Joe Briggs)*

"Who is that citizen?"
"That's my next-door neighbor."
"He looks as though his mind could stand a little laundering."

—*John McGuire (reporter Michael Ward) and bit player*

"Did you ever want to kill a man?"
"My son, there's murder in every intelligent man's heart."

—*John McGuire (reporter Michael Ward) and bit player*

Strangers on a Train 1951

"Young lady, there's no overlooking the fact that murder is on our doorstep. But let's not drag it into the living room."

—*Leo G. Carroll (Senator Morton) to Patricia Hitchcock (his daughter Babs)*

"Some people are better off dead. Like your wife and my father, for instance."

—*Robert Walker (playboy Bruno Antony) to Farley Granger (tennis pro Guy Haines)*

"She was a tramp."
"She was a human being. And let me remind you that even the most unworthy of us has a right to life and the pursuit of happiness."
"From what I hear, she pursued it in all directions."

—*Leo G. Carroll (Senator Morton) and Patricia Hitchcock (his daughter Babs)*

Opposite: Joe Briggs (Elisha Cook, Jr.) almost dies in the chair for the murder committed by Peter Lorre, the stranger with no name, shown here, who is *The Stranger on the Third Floor* (1940). Studded with expressionistic dream sequences, it is considered by some to be the first film noir.

The Street with No Name 1948

"You open that window again, I'll throw you out of it."
—*Richard Widmark (gangster Alec Stiles)*

"You gotta long nose, why don't ya keep it to yourself?"
—*Joseph Pevney (Matty)*

"Here, buy yourself a closetful of clothes. I like my boys to look sharp."
—*Richard Widmark (gangster Alec Stiles) to Mark Stevens (undercover agent Gene Cordell)*

Sudden Fear 1952

"Remember what Nietzsche said—'Live dangerously.' "
"You know what happened to Nietzsche."
"What?"
"He's dead."
—*Joan Crawford (playwright/heiress Myra Hudson) and Jack Palance (her gold-digging husband Lester Blaine)*

SUDDEN FEAR 1952

"I'M SO CRAZY ABOUT YOU I COULD BREAK YOUR BONES."
—*Jack Palance (two-timing Lester Blaine) to Gloria Grahame (Irene Neves, his equally perverse mistress)*

Opposite: When playwright/heiress Myra Hudson (Joan Crawford) discovers that her husband is not only two-timing her but is plotting to poison her for her money, she diabolically turns the tables on him in *Sudden Fear* (1952). THE TEEGARDEN/NASH COLLECTION

JOSEPH KAUFMAN presents

A NEW HIGH IN SUSPENSE MELODRAMA!

Joan Crawford
in
Sudden Fear!
PALANCE · GLORIA GRAHAME · BRUCE BENNETT
VIRGINIA HUSTO
TOUCH CONNOR
Produced by JOSEPH KAUFMAN
Directed by DAVID MILLER

Suddenly 1954

"If you think I have any qualms about killing this kid, you couldn't be more wrong. The thing about killing him, or you, or her, or him is that I wouldn't be getting paid for it—and I don't like giving anything away for free."

—*Frank Sinatra (contract killer Johnny Baron)*

"Show me a guy who has feelings, and I'll show you a sucker."

—*Frank Sinatra (contract killer Johnny Baron)*

"Funny thing—in the war you do a lot of chopping and you get a medal for it. You come back and do the same thing and they fry you for it."

—*Frank Sinatra (contract killer Johnny Baron)*

Sunset Boulevard 1950

"I always heard you had some kind of talent."
"That was last year. This year I'm trying to make a living."

—*Nancy Olson (script reader Betty Schaefer) to William Holden (screenwriter Joe Gillis)*

"Wait a minute, haven't I seen you before? I know your face."
"Get out."
"You're Norma Desmond. You used to be in silent pictures. You used to be big!"
"I am still big. It's the pictures that got small."

—*William Holden (screenwriter Joe Gillis) and Gloria Swanson (forgotten film star Norma Desmond)*

"I've made up my mind. We'll bury him in the garden. Any city laws against that?"

—*Gloria Swanson (forgotten film star Norma Desmond) to William Holden (screenwriter Joe Gillis)*

Opposite: Psychotic hit man Johnny Baron (Frank Sinatra), who has just shot lawman Tod Shaw (Sterling Hayden), brutally sets his broken arm as other hostages Pop Benson (James Gleason), Ellen Benson (Nancy Gates) and the boy Pidge (Kim Charney) look on in horror in *Suddenly* (1954).

103

Sweet Smell of Success 1957

"Can I come in, J.J.?"
"No. You're dead, son. Get
    yourself buried."
—*Tony Curtis (publicity agent
Sidney Falco) and Burt Lancaster
(columnist J. J. Hunsecker)*

"What am I? A bowl of fruit?
A tangerine that peels in a
minute?"
—*cigarette girl to Tony Curtis
(publicity agent Sidney Falco)*

"Steve shouldn't get mixed up
with no bimbo at his age."
—*bit player*

"Can you deliver?"
"Tonight. Before you go to
    bed. Cat's in the bag, and
    the bag's in the river."
—*Burt Lancaster (columnist J. J.
Hunsecker) and Tony Curtis
(publicity agent Sidney Falco)*

"My right hand hasn't seen
my left hand in thirty years."
—*Burt Lancaster (columnist J. J.
Hunsecker)*

They Drive by Night 1940

"Hey waitress, this steak's
    tough."
"Well, you can't send it back,
    you bit it."
—*truck driver and Ann Sheridan
(waitress Cassie Hartley)*

"Your liver must look like a
    bomb hit it."
"Well, you know what they
    say: live and let liver."
—*Ida Lupino (femme fatale Lana
Carlson) and Alan Hale (her
husband Ed)*

"Do you believe in love at
    first sight?"
"It saves a lot of time."
—*Ann Sheridan (waitress Cassie
Hartley) and George Raft (Joe)*

They Live by Night 1948

"Some say he's bad, but I say
he's bonny."
—*Cathy O'Donnell (Keechie) about
her prison escapee husband*

Opposite: *They Live by Night*
(1948), about a young
couple on the run from the
law, was director Nicholas
Ray's first film. It is based on
the novel *Thieves Like Us*,
the title under which Robert
Altman remade the film in
1974.

They Won't Believe Me 1947

"She looked like a very special kind of dynamite, neatly wrapped in nylon and silk. Only I wasn't having any. I'd been too close to an explosion already. I was powder-shy."

—*Robert Young (accused murderer Larry Ballantine) about Susan Hayward (his mistress Verna Carlson)*

Opposite: Playboy Larry Ballantine (Robert Young), wrongfully accused of murder, spies on an old girlfriend, Janice Bell (Jane Greer) and Trenton (Tom Powers) in *They Won't Believe Me*. Produced by Joan Harrison, who also produced some of Alfred Hitchcock's films.

The Thin Man 1934

"Would you mind putting that gun away? My wife doesn't mind, but I'm very timid."

—*William Powell (private eye Nick Charles)*

"The next person that says Merry Christmas to me, I'll kill them."

—*Myrna Loy (private eye Nora Charles)*

The Third Man 1949

"That's what I like about your books, sir, you can pick them up and put them down anytime."

—*Bernard Lee (Sargent) to Joseph Cotten (Holly Martins)*

"In Italy, for thirty years under the Borgias they had warfare, terror, murder and bloodshed, but they produced Michelangelo, Leonardo Da Vinci and the Renaissance. In Switzerland, they had brotherly love, they had five hundred years of democracy and peace—and what did they produce? The cuckoo clock."

—*Orson Welles (Harry Lime)*

"They want you to talk on the crisis of faith."
"What's that?"
"Oh, I thought you'd know. You're the writer."

—*Wilfrid Hyde-White (Cribbin) to Joseph Cotten (Holly Martins)*

Opposite: Noir icon Orson Welles as the mysterious and evil Harry Lime, who's lured his old friend, the innocent Holly Martins (Joseph Cotten), to bombed-out postwar Vienna in Carol Reed's *The Third Man* (1949). THE TEEGARDEN/NASH COLLECTION

This Gun for Hire 1942

"I want to know all about
  you."

"That's a big little word, all."

"Well, practically all."

—*Laird Cregar (crooked Willard
Gates) to Veronica Lake (undercover
agent Ellen Graham)*

"You're trying to make me go
soft. Well, you can save your
oil, I don't go soft for
anybody."

—*Alan Ladd (hired killer Philip
Raven) to Veronica Lake (undercover
agent Ellen Graham)*

To Have and Have Not 1945

"Who was the girl, Steve?"

"What girl?"

"The one who left you with
  such a high opinion of
  women. She must have
  been quite a gal."

—*Lauren Bacall ("Slim" Marie) to
Humphrey Bogart (Harry "Steve"
Morgan)*

"You know, you don't have to
act with me, Steve. You don't
have to say anything and you
don't have to do anything.
Not a thing. Oh, maybe just
whistle. You know how to
whistle, don't you, Steve? You
just put your lips together
and blow."

—*Lauren Bacall ("Slim" Marie)
to Humphrey Bogart (Harry "Steve"
Morgan)*

Opposite: Cold-blooded
psycho killer Philip Raven
(Alan Ladd) in *This Gun for
Hire* (1942), which had a
screenplay by pulp writer
W. R. Burnett and Albert
Maltz and was adapted from
a novel by Graham Greene.

THE TEEGARDEN/NASH COLLECTION

Top: Humphrey Bogart and
Lauren Bacall in the classic *To
Have and Have Not* (1945).

Touch of Evil 1958

"I'm Hank Quinlan."
"I didn't recognize you. You should lay off the candy bars."
—*Marlene Dietrich (fortune teller Madame Tanya) and Orson Welles (detective Hank Quinlan)*

"You're a mess, honey."
—*Marlene Dietrich (fortune teller Madame Tanya) to Orson Welles (detective Hank Quinlan)*

Uncle Harry aka The Strange Affair of Uncle Harry 1945

"Home is where you go and where they have to let you in."
—*George Sanders (John Quincy)*

"Old Sure Death, I call it. My own mixture. One pinch and you wake up being measured for a harp."
—*Harry Von Zell (druggist Ben)*

Underworld Story 1950

"I never asked you for a nickel, baby, did I?"
"You wouldn't have gotten it. You were never worth that much."
—*Dan Duryea (reporter Mike Reese) and gal reporter*

"Lakeville—you know, that's a good spot for you. A cemetery surrounded by bluebloods. One of those ivy-covered towns, shiny on top. You know what's underneath the ivy, Mike? Little crawling things. You should feel right at home there."
—*reporter to Dan Duryea (reporter Mike Reese)*

Underworld U.S.A. 1961

"Have you got anything in
    mind by way of a job?"
"A job?"
"Yeah, it's a word, meaning
    work."
*—Beatrice Kay (speakeasy owner
Sandy) to Cliff Robertson
(Tolly Devlin)*

"It was a pretty tough break
you had, being born in
prison and your mother
dying there."
*—Beatrice Kay (speakeasy owner
Sandy) to Cliff Robertson
(Tolly Devlin)*

The Uninvited 1944

"Between you and me and the
grand piano, I'm afraid my
father was rather a bad hat."
—Gail Russell (Stella)

Vertigo 1958

"That was where you made
your mistake, Judy. You
shouldn't keep souvenirs of a
killing. You shouldn't have
been that sentimental."
*—James Stewart (ex-policeman John
"Scotty" Ferguson) to Kim Novak
(femme fatale Judy Barton)*

Above: Tolly Devlin (Cliff
Robertson), the motherless
son of a hoodlum, with bar
girl Cuddles (Dolores Dorn),
another of society's rejects,
who befriends him in Sam
Fuller's bleak and violent
Underworld U.S.A. (1961).

The Web 1947

"Anything I can do for
    you?"
"Any number of things, but
unfortunately I'm here
    on business."
—*Ella Raines (secretary Noel
Faraday) and Edmond O'Brien
(lawyer Bob Regan)*

"When I'm worth forty
    million, I'm going to
    have a secretary who
    looks like you."
"Oh, my tastes are simple—
    twenty million will be
    quite enough."
—*Edmond O'Brien (lawyer Bob
Regan) and Ella Raines (secretary
Noel Faraday)*

"What if they're arrested for
    murder?"
"What are you talking about?
    Whose murder?"
"Yours, Charles."
—*Vincent Price (crooked tycoon) and
John Abbott (henchman Charles
Murdock)*

"Listen, I know a little place."
"I'm sure you do."
—*Edmond O'Brien (lawyer Bob
Regan) and Ella Raines (secretary
Noel Faraday)*

When Strangers Marry
aka **Betrayed** 1944

"Hey, that's a lot of money
    to be carrying around,
    Mr. Prescott."
"Only ten grand. I've carried
    ten times more than that
    without losing a dime. I
    don't believe in banks. I've
    tried them, you see."
—*bartender and Dick Elliott
(salesman Sam Prescott)*

While the City Sleeps 1956

"When you adopted me, you
wanted a girl, didn't you?
And he wanted a boy. Well,
neither one of you was
satisfied, were they?"
—*killer to his mother*

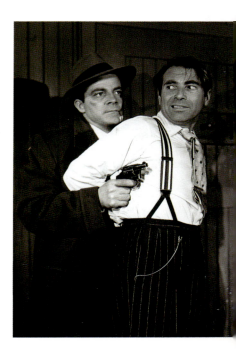

Above: Brutal police officer
Mark Dixon (Dana Andrews)
has the drop on mobster
Scalise (Gary Merrill), whom
Dixon is trying to frame for
a murder he himself
committed in *Where the
Sidewalk Ends* (1950). Otto
Preminger directed and Ben
Hecht wrote the screenplay.

115

White Heat 1949

"We ain't safe with no crackpot giving orders."
—*Steve Cochran (gang member Big Ed Somers)*

"I'd look good in a new coat, honey."
"You'd look good in a shower curtain."
—*Virginia Mayo (Verna Jarrett) and James Cagney (her husband, gangster Cody Jarrett)*

"I'm partial to blondes."
"Who isn't?"
—*Edmond O'Brien (undercover police agent Hank Fallon) and bit player*

"You wouldn't kill me in cold blood, would you?"
"No, I'll let you warm up a little."
—*Paul Guilfoyle (Roy Parker) to James Cagney (gangster Cody Jarrett)*

Opposite: In the prison yard, convicted felon Cody Jarrett (James Cagney) threatens fellow convict Vic Pardo (Edmond O'Brien), who is actually an undercover cop named Hank Fallon, in Raoul Walsh's *White Heat* (1949).

Above: Ad spot for *White Heat*. Cagney's performance as the disturbed, mother-fixated, and unpredictably violent criminal was one of his best.

The Window 1949

"I liked it, Mom, tasted kind
of like chicken."
"It was chicken."
—*Bobby Driscoll (Tommy Woodry)
and Barbara Hale (his mother Mrs.
Woodry)*

The Woman in the Window 1945

"There are only three ways to
deal with a blackmailer. You
can pay him and pay him
and pay him until you're
penniless. Or you can call the
police yourself and let your
secret be known to the
world. Or you can kill him."
—*Edward G. Robinson (Professor
Richard Wanley) to Joan Bennett
(femme fatale Alice Reed)*

"I'm not married. I have no
designs on you. And one
drink is all I care for."
—*Joan Bennett (femme fatale Alice
Reed) to Edward G. Robinson
(Professor Richard Wanley)*

"She's got something on her
conscience—but what
woman hasn't?"
—*Raymond Massey (district attorney
Frank Lawlor) about Joan Bennett
(femme fatale Alice Reed)*

You Only Live Once 1937

"Oh, go ahead—ruin your
life. Throw it away on a
worthless gorilla and end up
at my age with your future
behind you."
—*Jean Dixon (Bonnie Graham) to
Sylvia Sidney (her sister Joan
Graham), who is in love with Henry
Fonda (ex-con Eddie Taylor)*

Opposite: In *The Window*
(1949), a slum kid who is
always telling tall tales
actually does witness a
murder, but no one believes
him. The script is adapted
from the book *The Boy Who
Cried Murder* by the prolific
noir writer Cornell Woolrich.

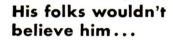

His folks wouldn't
believe him...

EVEN the police
wouldn't believe him...

BUT YOU'LL HAVE
TO BELIEVE WHAT
HE SAW...THROUGH...

R K O
PRESENTS

THE WINDOW

DORE SCHARY In Charge of Production

Starring BARBARA HALE • BOBBY DRISCOLL • ARTHUR KENNEDY • PAUL STEWART • RUTH ROMAN

Produced by Frederic Ullman, Jr. • Directed by Ted Tetzlaff • Screenplay by Mel Dinelli

R K O
RADIO
PICTURES

Daringly Filmed
ON NEW YORK'S TEEMING EAST SIDE!

INDEX OF FIRST LINES